COLLINS GEM GUIDES

BIRDS

illustration by
Martin Woodcock

text by

First published 1980

© Richard Perry and Martin Woodcock 1980

ISBN 0 00 458804 5

Colour reproduction by Adroit Photo-Litho Ltd,
Birmingham

Filmset by Jolly & Barber Ltd, Rugby

Printed and bound by Wm Collins Sons and Co Ltd,
Glasgow

Reprint 10 9 8 7

Contents

How to Use this Book

This book contains a painting of every species of bird likely to be seen in the British Isles, together with a short text describing the bird's appearance, voice and habitat, and indicating its approximate size by such terms as *very small* (tits) or *enormous* (swans), and by its length in centimetres from beak to tail. All the birds shown in a single plate are in relative proportion to each other. The symbol ♂ denotes a male bird, ♀ a female one; 'imm.' stands for 'immature'. A few species unlikely to be seen in Britain, such as the Alpine Swift and the Tawny Pipit, have also been included.

The simplest method of identifying a bird never seen before – a Nightjar perhaps – is to flick through the coloured illustrations until you reach a possible likeness, and then compare it with the text. From this it will be seen that the outstanding features of the Nightjar are that it is a crepuscular inhabitant of commons and woodland clearings, and that it has an unmistakable churring 'song'.

Identifying birds in the field is not easy, for their winter plumage often differs from their spring or summer breeding plumage. Moreover, the plumage of the sexes is often different, as in the case of the Blackbird, and that of the juveniles may differ from the adults'. Identification can be assisted by using binoculars – a pair with a magnification of 6x and a field of vision of 24 diameters gives a sharp image and bright colours and is therefore ideal for hedgerow birds, while for observing ducks, for instance, 8×30 is large enough without being cumbersome. For prolonged observation of, say, a distant seabird colony or flock of geese on a mudflat, a telescope with 20x magnification and 2in object can be used on a tripod. But ears are as important as eyes to the bird-watcher. Indeed many species, such as Warblers, can often only be identified by their different callnotes or songs, and a knowledge of these can only be acquired by personal experience in the field, or, less reliably, by listening to records.

Birds are much shier of human movement than of noise. Comparatively few will let you approach them closely over open country, but if your legs are hidden behind a low hedge or a stone wall you can get within a few yards of them. Weather is an important factor in bird-watching. Birds enjoy a moderate fall of rain and go about their business normally in wet weather, but in these conditions it is difficult to use binoculars. Most birds dislike wind intensely – the Mistle Thrush is an exception – and remain in shelter. A cold, calm day is ideal – a frosty snap stimulates birds to song and other activities, and a prolonged cold spell results in all sorts of birds turning up in unexpected places.

Introduction

An important aid to the identification of birds is a knowledge of their respective habitats, or the type of country in which they are likely to be found, though this may be different in the breeding season from that occupied during the winter, and a single species may be found in a number of dissimilar habitats.

Today, the characteristic breeding birds of town centres and built-up areas are, in addition to feral pigeons, House Sparrows, Starlings and Jackdaws, and in the summer House Martins and Swifts. In recent years these have been augmented by two Continental species. One, the Black Redstart, has discovered that bombed-out buildings and heavy industries provide ideal nesting sites; the other, the much more numerous Collared Dove, has found inexhaustible supplies of grain food around breweries, wharves and docks. During the winter months town centres are also the focal points of immense roosts of Starlings, containing tens or hundreds of thousands of birds, and of small roosts of Pied Wagtails.

Where there are parks and gardens the urban bird population is increased by Greenfinches, Chaffinches, Mistle Thrushes, Song Thrushes, Blackbirds, Robins, Wrens, Dunnocks, Blue Tits, Great Tits, Carrion Crows, Wood Pigeons and Tawny Owls, and during the summer by Spotted Flycatchers. If artificial lakes or ponds are available a normally shy bird, the Moorhen, is also attracted.

As suburbia passes into rural country with large gardens and small woods, Goldfinches appear, Magpies may be numerous, the first rookeries are seen, and there are Kestrels and Green and Greater Spotted Woodpeckers. Deeper in the country orchards and hawthorn plantations attract more Goldfinches and also Bullfinches, Hawfinches, Tree Sparrows, Lesser Spotted Woodpeckers and Little Owls, and hedgerows are the habitat locally of Cirl Buntings and more widely in the summer of Common and Lesser Whitethroats. More species of Warblers – Chiffchaff, Willow Warbler, Blackcap and Garden Warbler – inhabit overgrown hedges and copses, as do Nightingales. Pheasants nest in the hedge bottoms, and Rooks and Herons in the treetops. Farm buildings provide suitable nest sites for Barn Owls and Swallows, and Stockdoves nest in holes in old timber. Fields bordered by hedges are the domain of Skylarks, Corn Buntings, Yellowhammers, Partridges and Red-legged Partridges. Four kinds of Gull feed on pasture and arable land during the winter, together with Lapwings, Golden Plover, Rooks, Jackdaws and Starlings; in the summer Lapwings and Curlew nest in the fields, as do, in a number of localities, Oystercatchers and a rare Corncrake or Quail.

The more open kind of deciduous wood attracts far more species and individuals than do coniferous woods. In addition to many of those already mentioned, one can expect to find in them Jays, Tree

Pipits, Tree Creepers, Nuthatches, various tits, Redpolls, Wood Warblers, Redstarts, Sparrow Hawks, Woodcock and perhaps Buzzards; while conifers are predominantly the habitat of Goldcrests, Coal Tits, Siskins, Long-eared Owls and, in the Scottish Highlands, Crossbills, Crested Tits and Capercaillie.

New species appear on heaths, commons, brecks and downs – such as Linnets, Woodlarks, Redbacked Shrikes, Wheatears, Stonechats, Whinchats, Turtle Doves, Nightjars, Stone Curlews and Cuckoos laying their eggs in Meadow Pipits' nests. Cuckoos and Pipits are also numerous on the moors of west and north Britain. There too are Red Grouse, Short-eared Owls, Merlins, Hen Harriers and such nesting wading birds as Curlew, Snipe, Dunlin, Golden Plover and Greenshank.

Finally, the Scottish mountain-tops have their unique nesting population of Ptarmigan, Golden Plover, Dunlin, Meadow Pipits, Wheatears and Snow Buntings. In the craggy glens intersecting them are Golden Eagles, Peregrines, Buzzards,

Kestrels, Ravens, Hooded Crows and Ring Ouzels.

Red-throated and Black-throated Divers nest beside lochans on the moors, together with Wigeon, Teal, Goosanders and colonies of Common and Black-headed Gulls. Every moorland stream has its Dippers, Grey Wagtails and Common Sandpipers, and Oystercatchers and Ringed Plover nest on its shingle-beds. In the lower, slower running reaches of rivers Kingfishers and Sand Martins excavate nesting burrows in the banks. Lakes and ponds provide breeding places for Coots, Moorhens and Water Rails, various species of Grebes, Mute Swans and such duck as Tufted, Pochard, Garganey, Gadwall, Pintail and Shoveller. In and around reedbeds are Reed Buntings and Reed, Sedge, Marsh and Grasshopper Warblers, and in certain localities, such as the East Anglian fens and broads, Bearded Tits, Bitterns and the now rare Marsh Harriers. Yellow Wagtails run about the cattle grazing on freshmarshes, and Redshank and Snipe nest in boggy places. In recent years conservation and the establishment of special reserves have brought back as nesting species to watery places the Avocet, Black-tailed Godwit, Ruffs and Black Terns that

formerly bred in Britain but had ceased to do so.

Docks and harbours, estuaries, the seashore, especially saltings and mudflats, are the centres from autumn to spring of the largest aggregations of birds to be seen in the British Isles. They include Black or Grey Geese, duck such as Wigeon, Mallard, Shelduck, Eiders, Scoter and Long-tails, and such Waders as Oystercatchers, Curlew, Bar-tailed Godwit, Knots and Dunlin associating in flocks of hundreds or thousands on the mudflats, and smaller flocks of Turnstones and Purple Sandpipers probing among the reefs and banks of seaweed with Rock Pipits. During the summer, when the majority of these waders have emigrated to nesting grounds, the largest concentrations of seabirds are to be found in the terneries on saltings and islands, but especially on cliffs and offshore islands, where Puffins breed in millions and Guillemots, Gannets and Kittiwakes in tens of thousands, with lesser numbers of Razorbills, the larger Gulls, Shags, Cormorants, Manx Shearwaters and various Petrels. Offshore and out of sight of land large assemblies of birds are not often to be seen, apart from gulls following fishing-boats.

BLACK-THROATED DIVER
Gavia arctica

This diver can be distinguished in winter by its dark, unspeckled back and by its habit of rising to flap its short wings. When nesting on lochs in the western Highlands it can be identified by the purple-black throat and white neck-stripes of its breeding plumage and its wailing and mewing cries. Like other divers, they are most commonly seen in winter off the east coast. Large (65cm).

RED-THROATED DIVER *G. stellata*

The most commonly seen of the divers can be identified by its white-speckled back and thin tip-tilted beak usually inclined halfway to the vertical. When nesting on small lochs or even pools in the Scottish Highlands it has a wine-red neck-patch (appears blackish in some lights) and a grey head and neck; it can also be recognised by its quacking *uck-uck-uck* as it speeds like an arrow over the desolate moors to feed in the sea. Large (62cm).

GREAT NORTHERN DIVER *G. immer*

A larger bird with a more massive dagger-shaped beak than the other divers. It is also more frequently seen on the wing at sea – its long, drooping white neck extended far out from its quick-beating wings. An Arctic breeder, it has been known to nest in the western Highlands and can then be recognised by its black head and neck, chequered black-and-white back and by its yodelling *hoo-hoo-hoo*. Large (75cm).

DIVERS

summer

Black-throated Diver

winter

winter

winter

Red-throated Diver

summer

summer

winter

Great Northern Diver

summer / winter

GREAT CRESTED GREBE
Podiceps cristatus

In winter this duck-sized bird may be seen swimming in estuaries and coastal waters around the British Isles; in summer it breeds on reservoirs, gravel pits, meres and lakes in most parts of England and Ireland but only locally in Wales and Scotland. In winter it is blackish-brown above and satiny-white beneath with small black ear-tufts; in summer, the tufts are much more prominent and these, together with large chestnut-and-black neck-frills, which expand when the mated pair rear up in the water during courtship, make the species unmistakable. Grebes announce their presence in their several-acre nesting territory by a loud booming *kraa-oo*. Large (47cm).

winter

Red-necked Grebe

summer

summer

winter

Little Grebe

RED-NECKED GREBE *Podiceps grisegena*

A scarce though regular winter visitor from northern Europe to eastern coastal waters. It can be distinguished with difficulty from the Great Crested Grebe by its yellow-and-black beak, the absence of a white eye-stripe and often by reddening of the neck. Large (42cm).

LITTLE GREBE (Dabchick)
Tachybaptus ruficollis

The smallest and commonest of the grebes, found on ponds and lakes throughout the country and also in estuaries and bays in winter. In summer it is unmistakable with its rich chestnut-coloured cheeks and throat; in winter plumage it can be told from the much rarer grebes on pp. 16–17 by its explosive 'whinnying'. Medium (26cm).

summer

winter

BLACK-NECKED GREBE
Podiceps nigricollis

A rather scarce but regular breeding bird in Britain, found on a few ponds and lakes with plenty of aquatic vegetation, especially in Ireland; it is sometimes seen in large but ephemeral colonies of as many as 200 birds. In breeding plumage with black neck and golden-brown tufts of feathers fanning out down either side of its neck it is unmistakable; it has a soft *poo-eep* call though it sometimes utters a loud, rapid trilling chatter of notes. In winter, when it frequents coastal waters as well as lakes, it can be distinguished from the Slavonian Grebe by its thinner up-tilted beak, by its high forehead and crown, and by the less clearly demarcated black on the crown which reaches down well below the eyes to the ear-coverts, and by less white on the neck. Medium (30cm).

winter

summer

SLAVONIAN (Horned) GREBE   *P. auritus*

A much less widely distributed breeding bird than
the Black-necked Grebe, it nests in single pairs or in
small colonies on large semi-floating rafts of vegetation on lochs and pools in the northern Highlands
of Scotland. It is less shy than other small grebes and
can often be watched at close range during the breeding season when its plumage is a burnished copper
colour on the neck and breast, with a black neck-frill
or tippet and head adorned with golden horns. It is
more vocal when nesting than the Black-necked and
utters a variety of calls including a prolonged, low-
pitched, rippling trill. In winter, when it is less frequently inland than the Black-necked, it can be distinguished by its straight beak and the sharp contrast
between the black of the crown, which ends at eye-
level, and the white of the cheeks. Medium (33cm).

GANNET

GANNET
Sula bassana

A dazzling white, cigar-shaped bird, with a
1.50m spread of black-tipped wings, which
fishes by plummeting spectacularly from a
height of as much as 30m to crash-dive in a
shoal. In the autumn the adults are accom-
panied by blackish-grey juveniles and pied
immature birds. In summer nesting Gannets
mass in thousands on the flattish top of a
skerry or in serried rows on large drums of
seaweed along the ledges of some great cliff
face, which is noisy the day long with their
ceaseless croaking. Large (90cm).

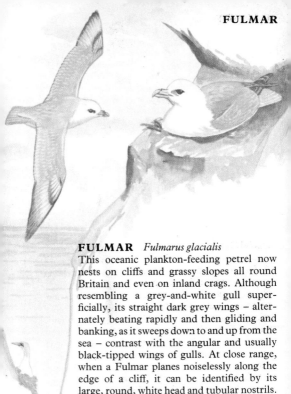

FULMAR *Fulmarus glacialis*

This oceanic plankton-feeding petrel now nests on cliffs and grassy slopes all round Britain and even on inland crags. Although resembling a grey-and-white gull superficially, its straight dark grey wings – alternately beating rapidly and then gliding and banking, as it sweeps down to and up from the sea – contrast with the angular and usually black-tipped wings of gulls. At close range, when a Fulmar planes noiselessly along the edge of a cliff, it can be identified by its large, round, white head and tubular nostrils. Medium large (46cm).

MANX SHEARWATER
Puffinus puffinus
This seabird breeds in large colonies, thousands strong, on islands and mountains on the west coast; non-incubating birds travel far and wide on fishing expeditions. It can be recognised by its contrasting plumage, black above and white below, and by its typical shearwater flight as it continually tilts its narrow rigid wings to one side or the other. On cloudy nights – the only time when the incubating birds are visited by their mates in the nesting burrow – the visiting bird can be recognised by its weird shrieking and sobbing cries, *chi-chi-cargo chi-chi-cargo*, while its mate makes a cooing noise like a pigeon. Medium (35cm).

STORM PETREL
Hydrobates pelagicus
This tiny petrel nests on islands off Britain's north and west coasts. Although exclusively nocturnal, they leave one in no doubt about their presence for incubating birds purr and hiccup for minutes on end from their pungent-smelling nests in the chinks of stone dykes, under boulders or in burrows excavated in soft soil. Storm Petrels are sooty black birds with white rumps, long wings and square tails, rather like House Martins (p. 146); their flight is characteristically fluttering and they often patter over the waves on webbed feet. Only when following ships or in stormy weather are they seen in coastal waters, as they feed far out at sea on plankton. Small (15cm).

21

SHAG

breeding

non-breeding

SHAG *Phalacrocorax aristotelis*

Shags and Cormorants, which both breed at various places around British coasts, are not easy to differentiate at a distance for both appear black, goose-sized birds, though the smaller, slimmer Shag is in fact a dark metallic green with bare yellow skin at the base of the beak (immature birds are pale brown) and is adorned by a recurved crest during the breeding season. In flight a Shag has quicker wing-beats, constantly jerks up its head, and seldom flies more than 30–60cm above the sea. It is an exclusively marine bird, roosting in caves and nesting on cliffs. Large (75cm).

imm.

adult breeding

CORMORANT *Phalacrocorax carbo*

These birds nest mainly on cliffs and skerries around Britain although some Cormorants nest on rocks and even trees on inland lakes; in winter, they are common in estuaries and far inland up rivers. At sea strings of Cormorants may be seen gliding in unison *en route* for their roosting cliffs or standing immobile for long periods on reefs or buoys with outstretched wings. The Cormorant can be identified at all seasons by the white on its face and chin (and in some birds on the head), and, during the breeding season, by a white thigh-patch; immature birds are brownish and have white bellies. Very large (90cm).

LITTLE BITTERN *Ixobrychus minutus*
Although this bittern breeds over most of western
Europe, it has only occasionally nested in East
Anglian reedbeds and is normally only a rare visitor
to the east and south coasts. It can be distinguished
from other heron-like birds by its small size and its
conspicuous whitish wing-patch which contrasts in
flight with the male's greenish-black back and head.
However, as it tends to skulk in reedbeds, clamber-
ing about the reeds like a gigantic warbler, or 'freez-
ing', with neck stretched upward in a camouflage
position, and is mainly active at dusk, it is more easily
identified by the deep croak it makes every other
second or so, which may be repeated for hours at a
time. Medium (35cm).

BITTERN *Botaurus stellaris*
The number of Bitterns nesting in Britain's
fen districts, mainly in East Anglia, varies
from year to year because they are extremely
susceptible to severe winters and loss of habitat. In spring and early summer they announce
their presence by a booming foghorn-like
woomp that can be heard over a kilometre
away. One may occasionally be glimpsed flying
for a short distance just above the reeds, when
it somewhat resembles a huge Short-eared
Owl (p. 130). Large (75cm).

PURPLE HERON *Ardea purpurea*

This heron very occasionally wanders to the east coast from European marshlands. In flight it could be confused with the Grey Heron, though it is smaller, even more attenuated and much darker; in addition, its wing-beats are quicker, the bulge in its neck lower, giving it a hollow-chested appearance, the wing colour almost uniform and the conspicuous long toes which stretch out beyond the tail can be seen at a distance. At rest the chestnut-coloured breast and black underparts are distinctive, and its long, extraordinarily thin, rufous-bronze neck is striped with black. Very large (77cm).

GREY HERON *Ardea cinerea*

A tall, gaunt, grey bird with a long, thin, yellowish neck, black-plumed head and long dagger-shaped beak which is found throughout Britain. It is characteristically seen peering over the top of a reedbed or a bank or poised motionless, with an S-shaped kink in its neck, waiting to make a lightning strike at an eel or 'flattie'. Its harsh, rasping *wartch* or *krarnk* is unmistakable as it leaves its nesting colony in the treetops and flies away with a slow, even, heavy flapping, head hunched into its shoulders and its long legs extended beyond its short, square tail. Very large (90cm).

HERONS

imm.

adult

Purple Heron

Grey Heron

LITTLE EGRET *Egretta garzetta*

This bird inhabits south European marshland, and is only a vagrant to Britain. It resembles a small, snowy-white heron with black legs, though in flight its bizarre yellow feet are conspicuous and its rounded wings beat more quickly; when feeding it makes sudden darting runs through the shallows and lightning thrusts with its sharp black beak. Large (55cm).

SPOONBILL *Platalea leucorodia*

Small parties of all-white Spoonbills are regular autumn-to-spring visitors to south and east England and sometimes winter in the south-west. Even when gliding and soaring with legs and long neck extended (unlike the similar-sized Grey Heron, p. 26) it can usually be recognised by the unique flat, disc-shaped, yellow tip to its long black beak. Large (85cm).

WHITE STORK *Ciconia ciconia*

Although once well established in Holland and Germany, this stork has rarely visited Britain. It flies slowly and deliberately with neck outstretched and legs trailing (like the Spoonbill) and may soar to a great height; it can be identified by its bright red legs and beak and jet-black flight feathers. Very large (100cm).

Little Egret

Spoonbill

White Stork

Bewick's Swan

Whooper Swan

♀

Mute Swan

♂

BEWICK'S SWAN *Cygnus bewickii*
A winter visitor to Britain like the Whooper Swan which it resembles. It can be distinguished by its smaller size, shorter neck and goose-like honking. Very large (122cm).

WHOOPER SWAN *Cygnus cygnus*
Herds of this straight-necked swan are winter visitors to Britain's lochs, bogs and coastal mudflats. They are noisy birds both when feeding and in flight and keep up a medley of bugling notes a little like those of the Cuckoo. At close range the extensive yellow on the beak can be clearly seen. Very large (152cm).

MUTE SWAN *Cygnus olor*
A British resident of about the same size as the Whooper Swan, but with a gracefully curved neck. Its great wings produce an unmistakable rhythmic clamour as it flies and its orange-coloured beak, with a prominent basal knob, is distinctive at close range. During the breeding season the male, which is usually silent, snorts and hisses and 'busks' its wings to warn rival males off the nesting territory where its mate sits on an enormous heap of water weed. Very large (152cm).

GEESE

Pink-
footed

White-
fronted

Bean

Grey Lag

32

GREY LAG GOOSE *Anser anser*
This goose is mainly a winter visitor to freshmarshes and saltings, grazing on fields and stubbles inland. It is a heavily built, greyish-brown bird with a long, flat head and a honking, deep-clanging *owch-owch*. Very large (75–87cm).

PINK-FOOTED GOOSE *A. brachyrhynchus*
This brown-headed goose, with a stubby black beak with a pink band, is the most numerous of the wild geese found in Britain. It breeds in the Arctic Circle and winters on west coast saltings and east coast estuaries. It may be spotted flying inland to feed on stubble or potato fields by its babel of high-pitched yelping metallic calls. Very large (60–70cm).

WHITE-FRONTED GOOSE *A. albifrons*
This goose winters mainly in western Britain and Ireland. It is the easiest grey goose to recognise, since the adults have white foreheads and heavy dark brown bars on their dark grey bellies; and a unique husky quavering *coor-rr-lew* call. Very large (65–75cm).

BEAN GOOSE *A. arvensis*
This is the brownest and least vocal of the wintering grey geese, occurring locally mostly in Scotland. It could be described as a large Pink-foot, though its long beak is black and orange-yellow and its legs orange. Very large (70–87cm).

GEESE

Brent Goose

Barnacle Goose

BRENT GOOSE *Branta bernicla*

Both dark and light bellied races winter on the coasts of Britain where *zostera* weed is found on the tidal mudflats. It can be distinguished from other 'black' geese by its sooty black head and neck, with a small white nick at the side of the neck, and by its guttural croaking. Large (58cm).

BARNACLE GOOSE *Branta leucopsis*

A winter visitor to the saltmarshes, links and grassy islands of the west coast of Britain. It is only slightly larger than the Brent Goose but can be distinguished by its snowy white face and belly, grey back and beagle-like yelping. Large (64cm).

CANADA GOOSE *Branta canadensis*

This species was originally introduced into Britain as an ornamental bird in the 18th century but it is now found wild in many parts and is the only 'black' goose to be found inland, grazing like the 'grey' geese on marshes and pastures near lakes and meres, nesting in small colonies. It can be recognised by its size (it is the largest goose in Europe), its brown plumage, black head and neck with extensive white cheeks, and its loud trumpeting honk in flight, distinct from other 'black' geese calls. Very large (97cm).

DUCKS

♂

imm.

SHELDUCK *Tadorna tadorna*

A resident on most British coasts where there are mudflats or sand dunes, it often nests in rabbit burrows, stone walls or bushes some kilometres inland. It is a rather goose-like duck, predominantly white with a greenish-black head, dark chestnut shoulders and belly-band, and black-tipped tail; in juveniles all the colours are very pale. At close range its magenta-coloured legs and beak can be seen; in the larger drakes the beak is prominently knobbed during the breeding season. Drakes make a whistling *tsew* noise, ducks a guttural *argg-argg*. It feeds by sweeping its beak through ooze. Large (61cm).

MALLARD *Anas platyrhynchos*

An ancestor of the farmyard duck, this is the best known and most widely distributed duck in all parts of Britain; in winter the resident breeding population is increased by enormous flocks of immigrants from Europe. The Mallard drake with its bottle-green or purple head and white collar is unmistakable, though when moulting it may resemble a brown duck or a juvenile; however, a female quacks hoarsely, the drake being restricted to a low murmur or thin whistle. Mallards are often seen at dusk flying with whistling wings to feed in ditches and mudflats. Large (58cm).

WIGEON *Anas penelope*

Tens of thousands of Wigeon winter in Britain on grassy saltings or mudflats and on inland lakes and reservoirs; they nest in the Scottish Highlands and locally southwards on hill lochs, moors and coastal marshes. The drake can be identified by its striking plumage – pale grey with a yellow-crowned chestnut head and lavender breast – when swimming, and by its white underparts and large wing-patches in flight. At a distance it continually whistles a loud musical *wrr-ee-oo*, while the rufous-brown duck with a stubby beak purrs and *chockaw-rrs* in reply. Medium large (45cm).

GADWALL *Anas strepera*

An almost exclusively freshwater duck which, although a resident, a winter visitor and a passage migrant, is distinctly local and uncommon; it nests mainly in parts of Scotland. The greyish drake and brownish duck are rather alike, and may be mistaken for Mallard (p. 37) with which they often associate. In flight the Gadwall's black-and-white wing-patch can be distinguished from the Mallard's purple-blue and white patch; at rest the drake Gadwall shows black above and below the tail. The Gadwall duck's quack resembles the Mallard's and the drake's nasal croak is seldom heard. Medium large (50cm).

PINTAIL   *Anas acuta*

This species nests locally in small colonies on the shores of lochs and islets mainly in Scotland; it is also found locally in winter in pairs or small flocks, chiefly on coasts though also on inland marshes. The Pintail is easily distinguished when swimming by its upright carriage and slim form, and in swift flight by its long slender neck, pointed wings and elongated pin-tail. Medium large (55cm).

TEAL   *Anas crecca*

This, the smallest European duck, is found in all parts of Britain, often at a distance from water. The drake has a curious brown and dark green head patterning and a golden patch under the tail; the brown duck can usually be distinguished by its glinting metallic-green wing-patch. Other characteristics are the rocketing, twisting flight of their small compact flocks and the bleating whistle and fluty piping of the drakes. Medium (35cm).

GARGANEY   *Anas querquedula*

An uncommon summer resident which nests mainly in east and south-east England in long grass or rush tussocks in marshy land. Although Garganey are unlikely to be seen with Teal, the two females can be distinguished by the Garganey's white instead of spotted throat, more pronounced eye-stripe and very dull green wing-patch; the drake has a prominent white stripe from the eye to the nape and a pale blue forewing. The Garganey's call-note resembles the sound of a wooden rattle. Medium (38cm).

DUCKS

Pintail

♂

♀

♀

Teal

♂

Garganey

♂

♀

SHOVELER *Anas clypeata*

Solitary pairs or small groups of these large-beaked ducks nest locally on fresh water throughout Britain; in winter, they are sometimes seen in shallow coastal waters dabbling their huge beaks in the water and ooze to sieve out small animals and aquatic plants. The drake is a striking bird with a gleaming dark green head (it appears black at a distance), an unusual yellow eye, white breast, chestnut belly and orange legs. The duck somewhat resembles a heavily built Teal but can always be identified by its top-heavy spoon-shaped blackish beak and pale blue forewing. Medium large (50cm).

POCHARD   *Aythya ferina*

A diving duck which nests locally in Britain, mainly in the eastern half from Scotland to southern England; it is more widely distributed in winter, when it is found in flocks of hundreds and thousands on inland lakes, reservoirs and large ponds. The Pochard dives for food to a depth of about 1m for 30 seconds or a minute, and like other diving ducks its colour pattern differs from that of surface-feeders. The plump drake has a grey back and flanks, a copper-red head and neck, black breast and tail-coverts, and white underparts; the duck is similarly patterned but drabber. Medium large (45cm).

TUFTED DUCK
Aythya fuligula

Like Pochard (p. 43), with which they associate, these ducks are essentially birds of lakes and reservoirs and nest locally mainly in coastal counties; occasionally in hard weather, when inland waters are frozen, they are found in coastal waters. The drake is a distinctive bird with its black head, back and breast contrasting with snowy-white flanks and belly, pale blue beak and legs, gleaming yellow eye and a hanging black crest at the back of the head which is very noticeable on a breezy day. The duck is similarly patterned but is coloured sooty-brown with off-white underparts and only a rudimentary crest. In flight, the white bar along the wing is conspicuous in both sexes. Medium (42cm).

SCAUP *Aythya marila*

A marine duck which occasionally nests in the north and west of the Scottish Highlands; when wintering offshore in 'rafts' of hundreds or thousands, individuals occasionally visit coastal ponds and lakes. Inland Scaup may be confused with Tufted Ducks for, although the drake Scaup has a grey back and black head and neck, these colour-distinctions are not obvious in flight when the wing-pattern of both species is similar; however, the Scaup has the heavy build of a Pochard or Mallard in contrast to the Tufted Duck's buoyant rotundity. The duck Scaup has a broad white band round the base of the beak but immature Tufted Ducks may also show some white, while immature Scaup may show very little. Medium (47cm).

♂ summer

♀

♂ winter

LONG-TAILED DUCK *Clangula hyemalis*

Known as the sea-pheasant by fishermen because of the drake's splendid white 'mane' and long black tail-streamers, this is the most marine of all the duck family; it winters off the east coast and the Scottish Isles but does not normally nest in Britain. When the sea is calm one may hear the drake's yodelling *caw-caa-calloo* and spot a flock rocketing over the waves. At closer quarters the pale pink band on the drake's short brown beak and the white half-moons round the eyes can be distinguished. The duck's tail lacks streamers but its small, steep-fronted head and dark cheeks make identification easy. Medium (52cm).

VELVET SCOTER *Melanitta fusca*

This species does not nest in Britain but is often seen in company with Common Scoters in the winter. However, flocks of Velvet Scoter rarely comprise more than 20 birds and one is more likely to see 2 or 3 diving for crabs in a shallow lagoon among reefs mainly on the east coast. Although also a black duck, it is considerably bulkier than the Common Scoter, shows a white wing-patch in flight, and has a curiously shovel-shaped orange-and-black beak, red feet and a small white patch beside the eye. The drab brown ducks and immature birds have 2 white facial patches varying in size and conspicuousness. In flight both duck and drake reveal triangular wing-patches. Medium large (55cm).

49

SMEW *Mergus albellus*

This saw-billed merganser is an uncommon winter visitor from north-east Europe; it is rare in Scotland and Ireland and is most likely to be seen in very small groups on reservoirs and lakes and occasionally estuaries in the southern half of England. Most Smews wintering in Britain are females or immature birds with grey-and-white plumage, chestnut-red heads and snowy cheeks and throats; at a distance they can be confused with one of the smaller dark brown and white grebes because of their habit of constantly diving. The drake Smew, the 'White Nun', is an almost pure white duck with conspicuous black markings on its face and a small black-and-white crest; however, as its wings are largely black it appears pied in flight. Medium (40cm).

GOLDENEYE *Bucephala clangula*

This duck is a locally common winter visitor to inland waters and estuaries and has begun to breed in Inverness-shire. Goldeneye are characterised by the conical shape of their heads; they are persistent divers and no other duck, except Teal (p. 40), spring into flight so instantaneously from the water, wheel round after gaining height and whistle back over the observer's head. The drakes are conspicuous with black upperparts, snow-white underparts and greenish-black heads with white patches below the eyes; in flight they speed up or down river with quick beating, loud whistling wings. On some northern estuaries drakes predominate; south of the Borders, ducks or immature birds with brown heads and grey backs are mostly seen. Medium (45cm).

RED-BREASTED MERGANSER

Mergus serrator

A British resident which nests in Scotland and Ireland on offshore islands or on the shores of sea-lochs; in the autumn and winter it is found in estuaries and around the coast of much of Britain. It is known as a saw-billed duck because of its long, very narrow, toothed and slightly hooked beak (blood-red in colour like its legs); this is used to hold the fish it catches after an underwater chase of up to 2 minutes. The rakish-looking drake can be recognised by its dark green head with a distinct, though wispy, double crest, and by its broad white collar and densely spotted rose-brown breast; the ducks and 'red-heads' (immature birds in winter) have slightly crested chestnut heads and necks. Large (57cm).

GOOSANDER   *Mergus merganser*

These birds winter on inland lakes, reservoirs and large rivers; in summer they breed in Scotland (but not Ireland), nesting in holes in trees and banks near wooded rivers and inland lochs. They occasionally visit the same estuary or bay as Red-breasted Mergansers and, since the ducks and the immature of both species have chestnut heads and necks, problems of identification may arise. However the heads of the Goosanders appear maned rather than crested (this is the most reliable distinction), their upperparts are bluish-grey and in flight they display square white wing-patches. Drakes are easier to differentiate, being startlingly white and creamy-pink birds with dark green maned heads and black backs. Large (65cm).

53

KITES

Black Kite

Red Kite

BLACK KITE *Milvus migrans*
There is no record of this kite breeding in
Britain and it has only been sighted a dozen
times during the past 100 years or so. This is
despite the fact that on the Continent it, and
not the Red Kite, is the common scavenger
and the most frequently seen of all birds of
prey, whether scavenging for dead or dying
fish along rivers or on the wing over forest
and steppe throughout Europe (except the
Netherlands and eastern Iberia). It is distinguished from the Red Kite by darker
plumage, a less forked tail and a more
Buzzard-like appearance. Large (58cm).

RED KITE *Milvus milvus*
For many years this kite's only breeding place
in the British Isles has been mid-Wales,
though it was formerly a very numerous scavenger in London and other urban areas. Its
present, strictly protected, habitat provides
50–60 adults with hanging oakwoods in
which to nest and roost; damp meadows and
wooded valleys in which to hunt for young
crows, pigeons, black-headed gulls, young
rabbits and moles; and most importantly, up-
land sheep-walks, since half its food consists
of carrion. Although its soaring flight resembles the Buzzard's its long, deeply forked
tail and angled wing present a different sil-
houette and its head is whitish. Large (61cm).

MARSH HARRIER *Circus aeruginosus*

A very numerous bird of prey in some parts of Europe, ranging low over the dense reedbeds to which it is almost exclusively restricted, it has been almost exterminated by persecution and loss of habitat in its former British stronghold of the Fens. Its larger size, broader wings and the absence of white on the rump distinguish male, female and immature birds from other harriers. Large (48–56cm).

HEN HARRIER *Circus cyaneus*

A rather owl-like harrier with very long wings and tail which is increasing spectacularly on north British moors as a result of afforestation and in the Orkneys as a result of protection. In other parts the brown immature 'ring-tail' with white rump-patch and black tail-bar is the most frequent bird of passage and winter visitor. Large (43–51cm).

MONTAGU'S HARRIER
Circus pygargus

The brown females of this kestrel-like harrier and of the Hen Harrier are virtually indistinguishable, though the immature Montagu's have reddish-brown underparts; however, since Montagu's is exclusively a scarce summer resident in southern Britain, confusion can seldom arise. Both males are pearl-grey with black-tipped wings; the Montagu's male is distinguished by a greyish rump and a black wing-bar. Large (41–46cm).

HARRIERS

Marsh ♀ ♂

Hen ♀ ♂

Montagu's ♀ ♂

juv.

adult

GOSHAWK *Accipiter gentilis*

A few of these huge sparrowhawks are now nesting again in some British woods though the majority have probably been released by falconers. Nevertheless they are always worth watching, whether hunting with a swift low flight made up of a few rapid wing-beats followed by a long glide, or dashing and doubling among trees with remarkable control and agility, or perched on a look-out tree at the edge of a wood. The female is the larger bird and with short rounded wings and a long barred tail resembles a very big female Sparrowhawk. Medium large (female 60cm, male 48cm).

SPARROWHAWK *Accipiter nisus*

This bird breeds in small numbers throughout Britain in wooded agricultural country; the use of insecticides as seed-dressings brought about the virtual extinction of it in the south and east of England in the 1960s. The male is slate-grey with barred reddish-brown underparts and conspicuously long yellow legs; the much larger female is grey-brown on the back and whiter beneath. Sparrowhawks soar high over their nesting wood with a harsh *squee-oo* cry and when hunting dash low through woods and skim the tops of hedges in pursuit of small birds. Medium (female 37cm, male 27cm).

BUZZARD *Buteo buteo*

This bird of prey breeds in 2 different habitats – sea cliffs and wooded valleys – in the western half of Britain. It is often described as resembling a small Golden Eagle but most Buzzards have white on their underparts. They can also be distinguished by their drawn-out mewing *peeyowow* cries while soaring for hours at a time or when disturbed on their nests. Large (52cm).

ROUGH-LEGGED BUZZARD
Buteo lagopus

A few of these birds visit Britain every winter from Scandinavia. They can be distinguished from the common Buzzard by whiter underparts, white tail with broad dark terminal bands, and white feathery legs in contrast to the Buzzard's yellow unfeathered ones. They hover frequently while hunting and can run quite fast on the ground. Large (55cm).

HONEY BUZZARD *Pernis apivorus*

This buzzard nests occasionally in large woods with open glades in the southern half of England; however, in a bad summer it may be unable to find enough of the wasp and bee grubs on which it feeds. It can be distinguished from other buzzards by its narrower wings, longer tail with broad dark bars on the underside and smaller head. Large (54cm).

BUZZARDS

Buzzard

Rough-legged
Buzzard

Honey Buzzard

OSPREY

OSPREY *Pandion haliaetus*

During the past 30 years Ospreys have begun breeding again near several lochs in the Scottish Highlands; elsewhere in Britain migrants occasionally visit lakes, fens and estuaries. The Osprey preys almost exclusively on fish which it seizes with its talons after hovering over the water and then plunging down feet first. With its dark brown back and gleaming white underparts it cannot be confused with any other bird of prey. Large (58cm).

adult

imm.

GOLDEN EAGLE *Aquila chrysaetos*
Found predominantly in the Scottish Highlands, the
Golden Eagle can be distinguished from the very
much smaller Buzzard (p. 60) by its immensely
powerful flight with the long primary feathers
splayed out and swept up; an immature bird can
be distinguished from the Sea Eagle (now very rare
in Britain) by its square white tail which ends in a
broad black bar. At close range the Golden Eagle is
unmistakable. Very large (79–88cm).

KESTREL *Falco tinnunculus*

This is the most numerous and widely distributed of
the British falcons, though in recent years very large
numbers have been killed by poisonous insecticides in south and east England. It is usually
easy to recognise because it spends much of its time
in a conspicuous hover flight on swiftly fanning
wings while searching the ground for a mouse or
beetle. Both sexes have reddish-brown plumage –
spotted in the male, barred in the female – and the
male also has a bluish-grey head, rump and tail.
Medium (35cm).

♀

♂

MERLIN

Falco columbarius

A not very common breeder which is found on moors
and bogs especially in Wales, northern England and
Scotland where it flies down Meadow Pipits, following their every twist and turn, and mounting a metre
or so above them before striking. In winter it frequents coastal saltings and freshmarshes. When
perched the dark brown female could be mistaken
for a Kestrel; the much smaller male, little larger
than a Blackbird, is slate-blue with heavily striped,
reddish-brown underparts. Medium (27–33cm).

imm.   adult

PEREGRINE *Falco peregrinus*

This falcon nests on sea cliffs or inland crags in the
Scottish Highlands. At a distance it attracts attention
by a high-pitched 'whickering' screaming, its almost
vertical dive as it preys on such birds as grouse and
pigeons and, in normal flight, by swift winnowing
beats of its long pointed wings interrupted by long
glides. At close quarters the male is slate-grey with
heavy black 'moustaches'; the large female is darker
and browner with heavy black bars on its pale underparts. Medium large (female 47cm, male 37cm).

adult   imm.

HOBBY *Falco subbuteo*

A Swift-like small falcon which is found in southern Britain in areas with woods (where it nests in the old dreys of squirrels or the old nests of crows, magpies, jays or sparrowhawks) and heath (over which it can hawk insects and small birds with marvellous agility and speed). It resembles a miniature slim Peregrine with narrower pointed 'moustaches' but can be identified by rust-red on the thighs and under the tail and by heavily streaked instead of barred underparts. Medium (32cm).

GROUSE

winter
Ptarmigan

summer

♀

♂

Red Grouse

PTARMIGAN *Lagopus mutus*

This species is restricted to the treeless mountains of the Scottish Highlands and is rarely seen below 600m even when deep snow covers the 'tops'. It can be immediately distinguished from the Red Grouse at any season by its white wings and belly; in winter the mottled blackish-brown or grey breeding plumage changes to pure white except for the black tail and scarlet eye-wattles, and the cock's black facepatch – a marking that distinguishes it from the Willow Grouse of Scandinavia. It can also be differentiated from Red Grouse by its unique crackling, croaking and belching call notes. Large (36cm).

RED GROUSE *Lagopus lagopus*

Although Red Grouse occur as far south as the West Country, and in Wales and the Peak District, they are predominantly birds of Scottish moors. A typical sighting is of a covey of heavy, dark, round-winged birds whirring and gliding downwind at breakneck speed, moving swiftly from side to side, before whirling over the brow of the moor. During the breeding season the cackling *go-back, go-back* of excited cocks leaping into the air sounds from all quarters, and it is possible to approach them closely enough to see their coppery plumage, the wattles over the eye and the white-feathered legs. Large (38cm).

69

BLACK GROUSE *Lyrurus tetrix*

A resident of wooded hill country, this bird is
found predominantly in Wales and Scotland
though also as far south as Exmoor; it feeds
mainly on the buds and shoots of pine, birch
and larch. The blue-black male Blackcock is
unmistakable but the female Greyhen could
be confused with the Red Grouse (p. 69),
though it is actually greyer with a white wing-
stripe and a forked tail; however, Black
Grouse rarely visit moorland. Unlike the Red
Grouse, they take flight silently and only
warble their dove-like *roo-kroo* when perched
in trees or at the spring *leks* when the cocks
display to the hens. Large (40–53cm).

CAPERCAILLIE *Tetrao urogallus*

Predominantly a resident of coniferous forests in the Scottish Highlands which occasionally breeds as far south as the Tweed.
Capercaillie spend much of their time on the
ground; they feed high up in pines on buds
and needles. The female is not unlike a Greyhen (female Black Grouse) but can be distinguished by a rufous breast-patch, rounded
tail and its much larger size (though this may
be difficult to see in the undergrowth). The
male is a turkey-sized bird with a massive
head and pale yellow beak, metallic dark
green throat and upper breast and an enormous tail. Very large (60–85cm).

GROUSE

Black Grouse

♀

♂

Caper-caillie

♀

♂

PARTRIDGES

PARTRIDGE *Perdix perdix*

This dumpy, short-tailed, grey and sandy-coloured game bird, with glowing orange-brown head and dark chestnut horseshoe blazoned on its lower breast, is distributed widely over the British Isles. However, modern farming techniques have resulted in this native partridge being reduced to fewer numbers than ever before in its history, and it is now comparatively rare in many areas of Britain. It can usually be recognised by its alternately whirring and gliding flight as it skims low over hedges. Except during the breeding season it is invariably seen in small coveys which roost together at night in open fields where their jarring *ker-wit*, *ker-wit* is a familiar sound. Medium (30cm).

RED-LEGGED PARTRIDGE

Alectoris rufa

Distinguished by its blood-red beak and legs, white gorget with black border, and black, white and chestnut barring on its flanks, the Red-legged Partridge is essentially a bird of the sandy heaths of East Anglia; however, since being introduced to Britain some 200 years ago, it has extended its range as far west as Wales and as far north as Yorkshire. Unlike the common Partridge it often perches on walls and fences and also runs more and flies less frequently; in addition its clucking call notes are higher pitched and throatier than those of the common Partridge. It nests in hedgerows, crops and on areas of waste land. Medium (34cm).

QUAIL *Coturnix coturnix*
This small game-bird nests more frequently in crops of grass and corn in the southern half of England than elsewhere but it is becoming increasingly scarce. It resembles a tiny buff-coloured Partridge (p. 72), but it is seldom seen, being reluctant to take wing; it is usually located by the constant repetition, day and night, of its unmistakable liquid call-note, long translated by countryfolk as *wet-mi-lips*. Medium small (17cm).

PHEASANT *Phasianus colchicus*
In most parts of Britain Pheasants are reared artificially for shooting but there are some genuinely wild birds particularly in northern England and Scotland. Wild birds survive in jungly swampy places most resembling the habitats of their Caucasian and Chinese ancestors; while those bred for game are characteristically found in hedgerows, arable fields and parklands. The Chinese male variety (introduced towards the end of the 18th century) has a dark green or purple head, scarlet wattles round the eyes and in most cases a white collar; the Caucasian variety (introduced possibly in Roman times but certainly by the middle of the 11th century) lacks the white collar. This plumage varies in the fieriness of the coppery markings. The female is a plain, less coppery brown. The explosive crowing *jarr* and noisy wing-flapping of Pheasants at dusk or when driven to flight is unmistakable. Large (male 80cm, female 60cm).

Quail

Pheasant

COOT *Fulica atra*

A duck-sized bird, the largest of the waterfowl on this page, which gathers in large squadrons. Noisy and quarrelsome, it is constantly skirmishing over the water in pursuit of rivals; its call sounds like a cork being drawn from a bottle. The chicks are black with reddish-orange heads and necks and become grey-brown and whitish juveniles. Adults are unmistakable with coal-black plumage set off by a white beak and forehead shield; their green legs end in enormous toes. Large (38cm).

MOORHEN *Gallinula chloropus*

Typically a pond bird, the Moorhen has a red face-shield and yellow-tipped beak, green legs with red 'garters' and white tail 'sails' which it habitually flirts. It is warier than the Coot but its explosive croaking may be heard intermittently from covert. Medium (33cm).

WATER RAIL *Rallus aquaticus*

A thin, brownish bird, with grey breast and back and black-and-white barred flanks, which is most likely to be seen in winter. Usually the only sign of its presence in a reedbed, overgrown pond or ditch is a cacophony of groans, squeals and miaous; though occasionally one may be glimpsed fluttering, with long legs dangling, into the nearest vegetation or pacing gingerly over the mud, probing with its pinkish-red beak. Medium (28cm).

COOT, MOORHEN, WATER RAIL

imm.

adult

Coot

Moorhen
adult

imm.

Water Rail

CRANE *Grus grus*

Cranes have become more frequent visitors to those fenland districts of East Anglia where they nested until the middle of the 16th century; and as they have begun to breed in Denmark they may do so again in Britain. They can be distinguished from herons (p. 26) by harsh trumpeting cries and, in flight, by the neck which is stretched out instead of hunched back into the shoulders. On the ground it can be recognised by the curved white stripe on the side of the head and neck, contrasting black face and neck, red crown and the drooping blackish feathers which obscure the true tail. Enormous (112cm).

GREAT BUSTARD *Otis tarda*
An attempt is being made to reintroduce this Turkey-like bird to Salisbury Plain where until early in the 19th century it bred in droves of 50 or more; elsewhere Great Bustards are now only very rare vagrants to Britain from the prairie cornfields and steppes of Iberia and central and eastern Europe. Their very large size, heavy brown bodies barred with black and long thick legs and necks make identification easy; in flight they appear mainly white with black-tipped widespread wings. The male can be recognised by its grey head and neck and white moustache-like whiskers; the females are much smaller. Huge (100cm).

OYSTERCATCHER

OYSTERCATCHER *Haematopus ostralegus*

These birds congregate in hundreds or thousands in winter on sea-shores, reefs, coastal mudflats and salt-marshes; in summer many pairs breed away from the sea, some far inland up northern rivers, scraping out a hollow which they line with small pebbles or shell fragments. They are conspicuous birds with black-and-white plumage, brilliant orange-red beaks and pink legs; in flight the broad white wing-bar and white rump form a white T on the back. Oyster-catchers attract attention by their incessant noisy piping *pic-pic* and rippling *kervee-kervee-kervee*. Medium large (42cm).

AVOCET *Recurvirostra avosetta*
Small numbers of Avocets visit the more southerly
estuaries and saltmarshes of Britain from Europe
every year, and colonies now nest regularly in the
bird sanctuaries of Minsmere and Havergate Isle
in Suffolk. With their loud yelping cries, snowy-
white plumage with black markings, long, slender,
uniquely up-curved beaks and very long grey-
blue legs which project beyond their tails in flight,
Avocets are unmistakable birds. Their feeding
habits are also distinctive as they sweep their long
beaks from side to side or in deeper water up-end like
ducks. Medium large (42cm).

RINGED PLOVER
Charadrius hiaticula

This is much the commonest of the 3 small waders illustrated here. It can be distinguished from other seashore birds by its black cheeks, black mark through the eyes, white collar, black breastband and orange-yellow legs. It feeds with sudden little runs and halts, uttering a soft *phooee*; in flight its long, tapering wings show a white stripe. Small (19cm).

LITTLE RINGED PLOVER
Charadrius dubius

This bird can usually be identified by its habitat, the reservoir or gravel pit. It is smaller than the Ringed Plover, does not show a wing-stripe in flight and has a high-pitched piping call. At rest the two species are not easy to separate, though the smaller bird has a white line above the black forehead and its legs are flesh-coloured. Small (15cm).

KENTISH PLOVER
Charadrius alexandrius

This is now only a scarce migrant through south and east England. Like the Ringed Plover it displays a white wing-stripe in flight but it is smaller and paler-coloured, with fainter, less extensive black head markings, blackish legs and beak, and a small black patch on its side instead of the Ringed Plover's breastband. Small (16cm).

PLOVERS

Ringed Plover

adult

imm.

imm.

adult

Little Ringed Plover

adult

imm.

Kentish Plover

PLOVERS

summer

winter

GOLDEN PLOVER *Pluvialis apricaria*

In winter these sharp-winged, golden-backed and silver-bellied birds with small beaks may be seen in flocks of hundreds or thousands around British coasts or, more frequently, on inland fields and fresh-marshes. They perform intricate flight manoeuvres and keep up a mass twittering; now and again one will break into the mournful *terphee-ew* it normally utters when joy-flighting above its nest. They breed on northern moors up to a height of 1000m, and in breeding plumage their cheeks, throats and underparts are raggedly black. Medium (27cm).

84

summer

winter

GREY PLOVER *Pluvialis squatarola*
This is a winter visitor and bird of passage to British shores, mudflats and estuaries. It sometimes occurs in 'trips' of a dozen, but is typically sighted alone on some unexpected part of the shore, while the soft, drawn-out *phee-ee-ee* calls of other plovers comes singly from different quarters of the mudflats. In winter plumage it resembles a darker Golden Plover but it can be recognised by its black eye-patch or, in flight, by black axilliaries or 'armpits' beneath its wings and black lines across its tail. In summer it is silver-grey above and black below. Medium (27cm).

LAPWING

imm.

adult summer

LAPWING *Vanellus vanellus*

Also known as the Green Plover or Peewit, the
Lapwing nests on grass and arable land throughout
Britain. A number of pairs usually nest in the same
field or marsh, and in spring their wild crying
wullock-wooee, zoowee-zoowee and the musical
throbbing of their broad rounded wings can be heard
all day long as they fight and tumble over their nests.
In autumn they flicker in black-and-white flocks of
thousands over freshmarshes and mudflats. The
male Lapwing has iridescent purple-green plumage
and a long wispy crest (short in the juvenile).
Medium (30cm).

summer

winter

TURNSTONE
Arenaria interpres

This winter resident on all coasts of Britain is usually found on mussel-scaps or reefs where it feeds on small shellfish. The small flocks can be recognised immediately by their unique method of pushing over weed or stones with their heads and stout black beaks in search of food, while trilling pugnaciously. They have distinctive short thick orange legs and usually have dark brown and white plumage. However, some birds retain their summer colouring and are mottled with rich tortoiseshell or purple-brown with a black breastband. Medium small (23cm).

WADERS

summer

winter

KNOT *Calidris canutus*
The Knot is an Arctic-breeding species which winters locally on the coasts of Britain especially in the east and north-west. It is usually seen in a flock, sometimes thousands strong, feeding on mudflats and reefs in dense grey 'carpets'. Most birds have pale grey and white plumage but some have a beautiful salmon-pink or orange tint on their underparts as a reminder of their spectacular chestnut-red breeding plumage. Knots are about the size of a Redshank (p. 98) but stockier and have much shorter black beaks and green legs. They are rather silent compared to other waders and usually only twitter softly in the air. Medium small (25cm).

summer

winter

SANDERLING *Crocethia alba*

A pearl-grey and white Arctic breeder which winters on sandy shores around Britain and occasionally on mudflats. It is usually seen in small 'trips' of 10–50 and is immediately distinguishable from other small waders by its habit of pattering very swiftly on short black legs along the edge of the waves to pick up plankton. It also runs in preference to flying if disturbed, with a sharp musical *swoo-eet*. In full winter plumage a Sanderling is the whitest of the waders and has black shoulders and wing-edges with a prominent white stripe. Some passage birds may be tinted on the upperparts with the buff or chestnut of their breeding plumage. Small (20cm).

CURLEW SANDPIPER
Calidris testacea

This uncommon passage migrant to mudflats and occasionally inland sewage farms is very similar to its frequent companion the Dunlin. However, it has longer legs and so appears larger. In most individuals the longer beak is distinctly curved (as are some Dunlins') and its white rump is conspicuous when it rises with a soft *twee-twee*. Small (20cm).

DUNLIN *Calidris alpina*

This is the commonest small wader. It can be seen in enormous flocks on the shoreline in winter, and nesting in saltmarshes, moors and mountains from Brecon and the Peak District northwards. Breeding and passage birds are recognisable by a black blazon on the lower breast, reduced in winter plumage to grey striping on the breast. It can be recognised by its whispered *tissee* call-note and, in summer, by a purring trill. Small (18cm).

LITTLE STINT *Calidris minuta*

This is the smallest wader seen on British shores in winter but it is uncommon. It resembles a diminutive Dunlin (its frequent companion), but lacks a black belly patch and has a distinctly rounded head, a short straight beak and a white breast; it usually pecks at mud, rather than probing like most wading birds. Very small (12cm).

summer

autumn

Curlew Sandpiper

Dunlin

winter

summer

Little Stint

imm.

SNIPE *Capella gallinago*
Except in parts of southern England, Snipe can be flushed from boggy or marshy places – flying high in swift but zig-zag fashion with a rasping *etch-etch* sound and the long, tweezer-shaped beak pointing downwards. It can also be recognised by a monotonous *chip-per* when perched on a fence, and, during the breeding season, by the humming noise made by its widely-spread outer tail-feathers as the circling bird dives steeply down over its nesting territory. Medium (27cm).

JACK SNIPE *Lymnocryptes minimus*
A winter visitor from Scandinavia which can usually be distinguished at a glance by its small size and short beak; its habit of rising silently and flying only a short distance (without zig-zagging) when flushed; solitary habits; and very bright ochre stripes on its back. Small (19cm).

WOODCOCK *Scolopax rusticola*
A winter visitor and a summer resident, mainly in woods, it is more heavily built than the common Snipe and rises silently with a twisting flight and downpointing beak. In the breeding season, the male is often conspicuous at dusk patrolling his territory while uttering bat-like *tzissick* noises. Large (34cm).

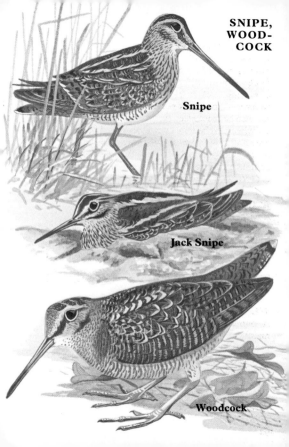

SNIPE, WOOD-COCK

Snipe

Jack Snipe

Woodcock

summer

winter

BLACK-TAILED GODWIT
Limosa limosa

This godwit has begun to nest again in Britain in places as far apart as Kent and the Shetlands; it is also a late summer and spring visitor to estuaries and freshmarshes. Large specimens stand almost as high as Curlew (p. 96); their legs are much longer than those of the Bar-tailed Godwit and stretch out well beyond their tails in flight. They can also be distinguished from Bar-tailed Godwits by their straight beaks, the white stripe on their wings, their very long necks and usually by a summery chestnut tinting on the head and shoulders. Medium large (40cm).

summer

winter

BAR-TAILED GODWIT
Limosa lapponica

This pale grey-brown bird is the godwit most commonly found wintering on British coasts. They may be seen manoeuvring in vast flocks over mudflats and sandy shores; in small groups or probing singly in wet sand for lugworms with long pink-and-brown beaks; or, if disturbed, flying away yelping their sharp *pip-pep* calls and leaving a maze of trident footprints on the sand. Although the male bird is burnished fiery orange in breeding plumage – the female is much duller – comparatively few with any red are seen in Britain. Medium large (37cm).

RUFF *Philomachus pugnax*
These birds, uncommon visitors to estuaries, marshes and sewage farms, have recently started nesting in Britain again. In the breeding season the males are unmistakable in multi-coloured ruffs and ear-tufts which they display to the much smaller reeves (females). In winter this silent bird differs from the Redshank (p. 98) by its narrow white wing-stripe and by an oval white patch either side of its dark tail. Medium (23–29cm).

CURLEW *Numenius arquata*
This is much the largest wader found on shores all round Britain and also nesting on moors and bogs. Apart from its size it can be identified by its long sickle-shaped beak, very long legs and a husky *courr-lee* call. A long drawn-out bubbling trill, preceded by a slow *whaw-up, whaw-up*, may be heard as the Curlew mounts steeply up and then makes a long glide down to its nest. Large (55cm).

WHIMBREL *Numenius phaeopus*
Though a few pairs nest in the northern Highlands and Islands the Whimbrel is better known as a spring and autumn coastal migrant. It can be distinguished from the Curlew by its 7-noted tittering contact call in flight, its shorter, less curved beak and the buff-coloured stripe on the crown of its head. Medium large (40cm).

Ruff

Reeve

♂

♀

Curlew

Whimbrel

REDSHANK *Tringa totanus*

The noisiest of all the waders, the Redshank is found on the coast and when nesting in marshes and damp meadows in most parts of Britain. It is distinguished by its plaintive *tew-phew-phew* which breaks into a frenzied shrieking when alarmed, its long orange-red legs and beak, a white rump, a broad white border near the back edge of the wings, and by a jerky flight. It bobs constantly and usually feeds in twos and threes. Medium (28cm).

SPOTTED REDSHANK *T. erythropus*

This scarce autumn visitor from northern Europe has a unique method of feeding in which 2 or 3 up-end themselves side by side in a few centimetres of water. Otherwise it is difficult to identify since most adults have lost their sooty-black breeding plumage, though their legs may still be blood-red; juveniles are brown like the Redshank. Medium (30cm).

GREENSHANK *Tringa nebularia*

This noisy white and ash-grey wader with an unmistakable *tew-tew-tew* call is both a passage visitor to coastal saltings and sewage farms, and a breeder in Highland bogs. It can also be recognised by its distinctive method of feeding, dashing through a shallow pool with its neck extended and the forepart of its head immersed in pursuit of small shellfish. Medium (30cm).

WADERS

Redshank

Spotted
Redshank

winter

Greenshank

COMMON SANDPIPER
Tringa hypoleucos

A summer resident which nests on shingle or in heather near rocky hill streams or lochs from Wales northwards. This dark olive-brown sandpiper with pure white underparts is very tame and will bob about within arm's length piping its shrill lisping *psee-pee-pee* incessantly. In fluttering flight it shows a white wing-stripe. Medium small (19cm).

WOOD SANDPIPER *T. glareola*

Although this sandpiper is known to have nested in the Highlands it is normally an uncommon passage visitor to sewage farms and freshmarshes. It can be distinguished from the Common Sandpiper by its white rump and from the Green Sandpiper by its more speckled back, a barred tail and, in flight, by its legs which stretch beyond the tail. Medium small (20cm).

GREEN SANDPIPER *T. ochropus*

Like the Wood Sandpiper, the Green Sandpiper has nested in the Highlands but is a commoner, usually solitary, passage visitor to marshes and freshwaters. This shy bird is easily identified by its clear musical *toos-leep* call as it towers up with twisting flight when disturbed and by its startlingly white rump which contrasts with its blackish back. Medium small (23cm).

WADERS

Common
Sandpiper

Wood
Sandpiper

Green
Sandpiper

ARCTIC SKUA *Stercorarius parasiticus*
A summer resident in the northern Highlands and
Islands, and a common autumn passage bird down
the east coast where it can be seen robbing terns by
following their every twist and turn until they drop
their fish. At their nesting colonies on moors and
islands Arctic Skuas are noisy birds, making wild
ringing *ayer-yah* cries and performing curious antics
when their nests are approached, waving their wings
and rocking about on their legs, hissing and screaming; they also mob intruders with stinging blows on
the head with their webbed feet. The Arctic Skua is
so sharply streamlined as to seem like a gigantic
Swift; it can be a uniform dusky brown or brown-
and-white, has a small head, very long wings with
pale patches, and projecting spine-like central tail-
feathers. Medium large (45cm).

GREAT SKUA *Stercorarius skua*

Also known as a Bonxie, the Great Skua breeds mainly on grassy islands in Shetland and Orkney where each pair takes possession of a mound or hillock, from which they can obtain a wide field of view. Unlike Arctic Skuas they are not very noisy birds but, from time to time, a pair will raise their wings, throw up their heads and repeat a *kee-yuk, kee-yuk* call; intruders are attacked fiercely and often struck heavily on the head by the bird's feet. To get food for their young Great Skuas chase Gannets and gulls and force them to disgorge fish; for their own food they kill smaller seabirds and also suck eggs. They are very heavy-bodied birds, larger than Herring Gulls (p. 107), with dark ruddy plumage streaked with buff, and a silvery patch on their broad rounded wings. Large (57cm).

GULLS

summer

winter

imm.

BLACK-HEADED GULL *Larus ridibundus*
This is the commonest gull found inland in all seasons. It nests in colonies of thousands of pairs on lake islands, shingle banks, marshes, bogs, sandhills and lochs keeping up an incessant clangour of harsh cawing. It can be identified from other gulls by its dark red beak and legs, the broad white border of the fore-edge of its wings, and its dark brown hood which is lost in winter except for a smudge or two on its face. Juveniles have mottled brown backs, white tails terminating in a black bar and yellowish legs. Medium (38cm).

imm.

summer

winter

LITTLE GULL *Larus minutus*

This is a regular though scarce autumn and winter
visitor to east and south coasts of England, from
eastern Europe. In buoyant Tern-like flight it appears only half the size of the Black-headed Gull; it
shows no black on the upper surfaces of the wings
though the undersurfaces are dark. However, most
of those visiting British shores are immature with
slanting black bars across the wings, forming a striking zig-zag pattern, and have black beaks and pink
legs. In summer the adult hood is jet black, in winter
white with black patches. Medium (28cm).

LESSER BLACK-BACKED GULL

Larus fuscus

This gull is mainly a summer resident which nests in colonies of thousands on lochs, moors and bogs both inland and on the coast – though not usually on steep cliff faces like Herring Gulls. It is distinguished from the latter by its pale or dark slate-grey instead of silvery-grey back and wings and from the Great Black-backed Gull by its smaller size and yellow legs. In immature plumage most large gulls are striped and mottled with black, grey and brown, though this species tends to be darker than similar-sized Herring Gull. Large (53cm).

HERRING GULL *Larus argentatus*

This is the commonest large gull around British coasts at all seasons and it also roosts in immense numbers on inland reservoirs. Its huge nesting colonies are mainly scattered around coastal cliffs and islands, though some birds nest on buildings. Nesting colonies ring to the birds' incessant howling *gerwyer*, not as deep-toned as the call of the Lesser Black-back, and the repeated *quee, quer-wew* of a mated pair answering each other. Its large size, angled yellow beak with a red spot, and pale pink legs distinguish it from the Common Gull (p. 111) and the Kittiwake (p. 110). Large (55cm).

GULLS

imm.

adult

GLAUCOUS GULL *Larus hyperboreus*

This huge heavy-bodied and broad-winged Arctic
gull, which in some cases may be larger than the
Great Black-back, is mainly a visitor to the east coast
in hard winters, though it regularly visits Shetland.
It can be recognised by the very pale grey of its
back and wings with pure white flight-feathers, and
its gleaming straw-coloured beak, though the majority on British coasts are pinkish immature birds,
mottled and streaked with sandy-coloured bars and
flecks, and dark pink beaks. It is an extraordinarily
silent bird as it planes and flaps ponderously along
the cliffs and tide-line. Large (65–80cm).

GREAT BLACK-BACKED GULL
Larus marinus
Though some Great Black-backs nest on inland lochs and moors the majority nest by the sea especially on the tops of stacks and islets. Few colonies contain more than a couple of hundred pairs, but the deep-toned barking *aw-oo* and *uggha-uggha* coming from even a small colony is an impressive sound. During the winter these big gulls gather to rest on sandbanks in flocks of several hundred. As large as a Grey Lag Goose, the Great Black-back has an intensely black back and wings (edged with white), and pale pink legs. Large (73cm).

imm.

imm.

adult

KITTIWAKE   *Rissa tridactyla*

In winter Kittiwakes are almost exclusively sea-going and rarely come inshore except to scavenge from fishing boats or in stormy weather; in summer they nest in thousands, with incessant *wick-gewer, wick-gewer* cries, on ledges and in niches on cliff faces, affixing nest cups to the slightest protuberances. They can be distinguished from other grey gulls by the absence of white 'mirrors' on the black tips of their long grey wings, by their blackish-brown legs, yellow beak and dark eyes, and by their flight, the wildest of all the gulls, as they bank this way and that cutting the waves with their wing-tips. Immature birds have a black yoke across the neck and a black band slanting across the wings. Medium (41cm).

summer

winter

COMMON GULL *Larus canus*

A well-distributed gull found on seashores, estuaries and inland pastures; it is never far offshore except when migrating. It breeds almost entirely in Scotland and Ireland, more commonly inland in small colonies on moor lochs than on grassy cliffs or offshore islands; nesting birds are not so incessantly noisy as other colonies of gulls but can be identified by the shrill *gee-yah, gee-yah* cries. It is about the same size as a Kittiwake but can be immediately recognised by its greenish-yellow beak and legs. Immature birds can be distinguished from the much larger Herring Gull by a narrower black band on the white tail; juveniles are predominantly grey-brown with a blackish beak and flesh-coloured legs. Medium (41cm).

winter

summer

ROSEATE TERN *Sterna dougallii*
The number of Roseate Terns breeding in
coastal colonies or as individuals among other
species of tern is decreasing in England, Scotland and Wales, though less quickly in Ireland. It can be distinguished on the wing
from other similar-sized red-legged terns, the
Common and the Arctic (pp. 114–15), by its
harsh cawing *caa-aa* and ringing *chu-vee* call-
notes. It can also be identified by its black
beak, whiter plumage with a rosy flush on the
breast (though this is lost during the breeding
season) and its very long tail-streamers which
extend well beyond the closed wing-tips.
Medium (37cm).

summer

SANDWICH TERN
Sterna sandvicensis
This large dazzlingly white bird with a shaggy black cap and yellow-tipped beak is the easiest tern to recognise; as with other terns, a white patch may appear on the forehead as the summer progresses. Its harsh grating *kroo-eech* call is also distinctive. Sandwich Terns typically breed in colonies on sand-spits or rocky islets, occasionally on saltings and the gravelly shores of inland lakes; again, like other terns, they are erratic nesters, concentrating in large numbers in a certain locality one year and completely deserting it the next. Medium large (40cm).

winter

summer

COMMON TERN *Sterna hirundo*
Terns can be distinguished from gulls by their smaller size, forked tails, black caps and habit of diving for fish. However, it is not easy to distinguish between Common and Arctic Terns, though the Common Tern usually has a black tip to its vermilion beak in the breeding season. Common Terns breed all round the British coast, often in company with Arctic Terns, in dense colonies that may include thousands of pairs; they nest in similar habitats to Sandwich Terns (p. 113). They are aggressive birds and will mob an intruder, striking him on the head with their sharp beaks, while scolding with a prolonged screaming *quee-arrr*. Medium (35cm).

winter

summer

ARCTIC TERN *Sterna paradisaea*

Although this tern is difficult to distinguish from the Common Tern, it can be identified by its shorter legs when perched, a duskier breast, longer tail-streamers projecting a little beyond the closed wing-tips and, in the breeding season, by its coral-red or puce beak which usually lacks the Common Tern's black tip; in winter both terns have blackish beaks. In addition, while both terns utter a more or less similar *quee-arrr*, the Arctic Tern has a whistling *pee-wee* cry and, when mobbing intruders at nesting colonies, a distinctive chattering series of notes like castanets. Very few pairs of Arctic Terns breed in the southern half of England. Medium (37cm).

LITTLE TERN *Sterna albifrons*

This delightful little bird, much the smallest of the marine terns, is becoming increasingly scarce as a breeding bird on British coasts. The individual pairs of the small scattered colonies are found strung out along the length of a beach where they scratch out bare hollows in the sand or fine shingle for nests. The Little Tern attracts attention with its sharp *whuit* call note as it hawks up and down a tidal creek, hovering every few metres with its long slender wings arching above its back before it dives into the water to capture a small fish with its black-tipped yellow beak. Its small size, yellow beak and the white forehead distinguish it from other terns though when other terns begin to moult at midsummer they also develop whitish foreheads. Medium small (24cm).

winter

summer

BLACK TERN
Chlidonias niger

This tern is a not very common visitor to coastal marshes and inland sewage farms though it has recently begun to breed again in Britain after a break of over 100 years. Unlike other British terns, the Black Tern is an insect-feeding marsh bird; it is characteristically seen flying to-and-fro over water, dipping gracefully down to pick off insects but very rarely plunging into the water or even touching it. In summer plumage it has a slate-grey back and black head and underparts, except for a conspicuous white patch under the tail, and dark red-brown legs. Immature birds have white foreheads, shoulder-patches and underparts. It is a rather silent bird except when in large breeding colonies with floating nests in the shallows. Medium (24cm).

AUKS

summer

winter

Bridled Guillemot

GUILLEMOT *Uria aalge*

Two races of this auk breed on cliff faces and stacks around Britain in colonies of thousands. One race which has almost black upperparts and white bellies is found on Scottish cliffs; the other, found further south, has paler chocolate-brown upperparts; another variety, the Bridled Guillemot, has white eye-rings and cords and is seen in small numbers. In winter Guillemots' cheeks and throats turn white and they spend the season at sea where their characteristic whirring flight and long, thin, pointed beaks distinguish them from other auks. Medium (42cm).

summer

winter

BLACK GUILLEMOT *Cepphus grylle*

A resident of Ireland and Scotland which is most uncommon on English coasts; if it does stray to England it is usually in its winter plumage with a mainly white head and belly and its back laced and barred with blackish-grey and white. In summer its plumage is dark brown except for a broad white patch on the wings, coral-red legs and a scarlet interior to the black beak. It is distinguished from the Guillemot by its size, its very high-pitched piping, and its habits of nesting in single pairs, swimming in long files of 20, 30 or more, and of spinning around one another in courtship. Medium (34cm).

RAZORBILL *Alca torda*

This auk nests in scattered colonies in cracks in cliffs or in burrows under boulders on western and northern British coasts. At their nesting stations Razorbills snarl harshly as they shuffle about the tops of boulders on the full length of their legs or alight from the sea with half-a-dozen small fish held crosswise in their beaks for the single nestling. A Razorbill is the same size as a Guillemot (p. 118) but intensely black-and-white with a pointed tail and a large, deep, compressed beak crossed by a white groove, with another white groove from the base of the beak to the eye. Medium (40cm).

PUFFIN *Fratercula arctica*

Though now drastically reduced in numbers, this black-and-white auk nests in colonies of hundreds of thousands on grassy cliffs and small islands on western and northern coasts of Britain. The Puffin is smaller and tubbier than a Razorbill or Guillemot (p. 118), and has an unmistakable huge conical red, orange and bluish-grey beak, and orange-red legs. A typical view of a puffinry is of thousands of comical little sea-parrots standing erect outside their burrows, with which the ground is pitted, or padding to and fro, while others are continually alighting with rows of tiny silvery fish held crosswise and head-to-tail in powerful beaks; however, Puffins are silent birds, and one seldom hears more than a sepulchral caw from beneath one's feet. Medium (30cm).

STOCKDOVE *Columba oenas*

A British resident, especially in parkland and on sandy heaths, which is usually seen in pairs; it nests in such varied sites as hollow trees, rabbit burrows, sea cliffs and inland crags. It is more numerous than it appears to be because its coughing *coo-wugh, coo-wugh* is seldom heard even during the nesting season. It is much smaller than the Wood Pigeon and distinguished by a shorter tail and the absence of white on the wings and tail. Medium (33cm).

WOOD PIGEON (Ringdove)
Columba palumbus

The commonest pigeon in most parts of the British Isles, it is often seen feeding in flocks of hundreds or thousands in beechwoods and fields of young corn. It is a heavily built bird with a notably small head, conspicuous white wing-bars, a strong clipping flight, and a repetitive cooing – 'take two coos, boo-boo' – when perched; it nests at any time and in a variety of sites. Medium (41cm).

ROCK DOVE *Columba livia*

This bird is now found only on the extreme north and north-west coasts of Scotland, the Northern Isles, the Hebrides and Ireland, and even in these places it is probably largely interbred with the feral domestic pigeon. It nests in crannies and caves in cliffs and feeds on nearby fields. Its plumage and voice are identical to the domestic Blue Rock Pigeon's; it lacks the black wing-tips of the Stockdove and has a wild, dashing flight. Medium (33cm).

PIGEONS

Stockdove

Wood Pigeon

Rock Dove

COLLARED DOVE
Streptopelia decaocto

During the past 25 years this pinkish-grey dove, originally an inhabitant of Asia, has spread over much of western Europe, colonising towns, villages and farms throughout Britain wherever it can pick up grain. The male may be seen on an overhead power cable making a deep *coo-coo-coo*, with the accent on the second *coo*, and zooming down to alight beside its mate with a buzzing note. It can be identified by the narrow black half-collar round its nape. Medium (28cm).

TURTLE DOVE *Streptopelia turtur*
A summer resident only, which is found mainly in south and east England and the Midlands; it winters in tropical Africa. Unlike the Collared Dove, it feeds mainly on the seeds of weeds and grasses. In places where both species are present the Turtle Dove can be distinguished by the black-and-white patch at the side of its neck, and by its purring 'song' as it mounts steeply with a slow flapping flight from a hawthorn hedge or orchard tree and then glides down with its white-tipped tail fanned out. Medium (28cm).

CUCKOO

imm.   adult

CUCKOO *Cuculus canorus*
With its pointed wings, long
tail and barred bluish-grey
plumage the Cuckoo could be
confused with a hawk; the
male's familiar call is unique,
the female's is a rather in-
frequent 'water-bubbling' trill. Cuckoos are particularly numerous on commons and moorlands, for
there the female can lay her dozen eggs in the nests of
Meadow Pipits. Other common foster-species are
the Dunnock, Reed Warbler and Pied Wagtail. Each
individual female Cockoo uses the same host-species
throughout her life, always laying eggs which closely
resemble those of the host. The young Cuckoo is
brown-barred with a distinctive white patch on its
nape. Medium (32cm).

NIGHTJAR *Caprimulgus europaeus*

This elusive bird is becoming increasingly local over commons and woodland clearings in Britain. Since it does not fly until dusk (to hawk moths and dorbeetles with its small beak but very large gape), it must be located by its interminable churring 'song', which sounds like the distant purr of a 2-stroke motorcycle. Rarely, it may be seen in the daytime, perched *along* a branch instead of across it or sitting on its 2 eggs in a scrape on a brackeny path, when its barred and mottled grey, brown and buff plumage renders it almost invisible. Medium (26cm).

BARN OWL   *Tyto alba*

Once found in most parts of Britain, this owl is becoming scarcer as farming techniques change and the large trees and old-fashioned barns in which it nests disappear. It is perhaps best known for its prolonged eerie screech and snoring hunting call and is most usually seen at dusk when it emerges to seek voles, rats and, to a lesser extent, small birds for food. In the half-light it appears as a ghostly snow-white bird with a round furry head and black eyes in a white face; in daylight – and in some areas it also hunts by day – it can be seen that only the underparts are pure white, the upperparts being mottled from faintest orange to burnished copper, shading to purplish-grey. Large (34cm).

TAWNY OWL   *Strix aluco*

This is the most widely distributed of all British owls, though absent from Ireland, and is found in many habitats from large town suburbs with hollow trees in parks and gardens to the extreme north of Scotland. It is most frequently identified by its quavering hooting and staccato *kee-veck* hunting note as it rarely begins to hunt before nightfall. Occasionally it may be chivvied out during the day from the tree where it is roosting by a scolding band of birds; it can be recognised by its dark, heavily built form with a very large round head, a mottled and streaked brown-to-greyish body, and broad rounded wings which it flaps with slow beats. Large (38cm).

OWLS

Barn Owl

Tawny Owl

LITTLE OWL   *Athene noctua*
Since its introduction to the Midlands from the Continent in 1889, this small mottled cream and grey-brown owl has spread to farmland, sand dunes and other areas in England, Wales and the Scottish Borders. It is often seen during the day bobbing and bowing on the ground or a perch with fierce, staring yellow eyes and square white 'goggles'. Medium (21cm).

LONG-EARED OWL   *Asio otus*
This is an exclusively nocturnal bird and is thus the least observable of all the owls though it is found throughout the British Isles in very localised habitats of coniferous woods; it is the only owl to breed in Ireland. This buff and grey-brown bird, with its long ear-tufts usually erect, may occasionally be seen during the day drawn up on a branch close against the bole of a tree; in the nesting season it can be located by a soft, tremulous yodelling. Large (34cm).

SHORT-EARED OWL   *Asio flammeus*
This owl hunts by day and is most commonly seen in the autumn and winter on coastal marshes and dunes; it nests very locally on moors and in young plantations in various parts of Britain. With its habit of soaring and gliding on notably long wings it could be mistaken for a bird of prey, but it has an owl's face and head, blazing yellow eyes and noiseless, buoyant flight; its ear-tufts are not always obvious. Large (38cm).

OWLS

Little
Owl

Long-eared
Owl

Short-eared
Owl

SWIFT *Apus apus*
An exclusively aerial bird, except when at its nest hole under the eaves of a building, the sooty-brown Swift, cutting black arcs across the sky on scimitar-shaped wings, could not be mistaken for any other British bird. Unlike other aerial birds such as the Swallow or House Martin, it may be seen chasing in screaming packs at breakneck speed down streets and round houses, or wheeling higher and higher into the summer dusk until it can no longer be seen or heard. Swifts return to Britain from wintering in South Africa in April or May and by August or September the majority have already left. Medium (17cm).

ALPINE SWIFT

Apus melba

Once in a lifetime an Alpine Swift, wandering from its home in southern Europe, might be spotted in Britain. Although it has the same scythe-shaped wings and forked tail as the Common Swift, it would be easily recognised by its habit of gliding more frequently in flight, its larger appearance, its pale brown colour with a white chin (barely visible in the Common Swift), white underparts and broad, buff-coloured breastband. However, one is unlikely to hear its distinctive, more musical trilling call, since it is usually silent away from its nesting haunts in the mountains. Medium (21cm).

BEE-EATER

BEE-EATER *Merops apiaster*

This rainbow-coloured bird is an infrequent visitor to Britain from southern Europe. Apart from its brilliant yellow, green and chestnut-gold colour, it attracts attention by its long curving beak, the projecting central feathers of the long blue-green tail, its incessant liquid call-notes, and, when in swallow-like flight, by its speed in pursuit of insects. In Europe, where its habitat is open country with scattered trees or telegraph poles, it nests colonially in holes in sandpits or river banks. Medium (28cm).

KINGFISHER *Alcedo atthis*

With its scintillating blue-green back, salmon-red
underparts, plum-coloured dagger-shaped beak and
red feet, a Kingfisher cannot be confused with any
other bird. It is also unmistakably characterised by
its piercing whistles as it speeds low over a river or
canal at 45mph or dives from an overhanging branch
into shallow water to catch a minnow. The nest
tunnel is excavated by the parents to a depth of from
25 to 55cm in the side of the bank a metre or more
above the stream's normal level; its entrance can be
spotted by the white excreta around the opening.
Medium (16cm).

ROLLER

ROLLER *Coracias garrulus*

This bird inhabits scrubland and forests in south, central and eastern Europe, in districts where old timber, ruins or crags provide nesting holes. On the infrequent occasions when it wanders to Britain it is unlikely to be overlooked since this Jackdaw-sized bird is pale azure-blue with a bright chestnut back! In addition its wings, when spread in slow, buoyant flight, are turquoise-blue – a colour shared only by the Jay among British birds. The Roller also makes itself conspicuous by its habit of boomeranging out, like some huge flycatcher, from its perch on overhead wires or other vantage point in pursuit of insects, and by tumbling and turning somersaults in aerial display. Medium (30cm).

HOOPOE *Upupa epops*

Although Hoopoes visit southern Britain every spring, they only occasionally stay to nest in holes in old timber, in parkland or orchards. Few such visitors can be missed, for with its pinkish-brown plumage, black-and-white bars on rounded wings and tail, and butterfly-like flight this unmistakable bird resembles a tiger-moth the size of a Jackdaw. Its long curved beak and erectile, black-tipped, pink crest, which can be spread like a fan, are also distinctive. Medium (28cm).

BLACK WOODPECKER
Dryocopus martius
This magnificent Rook-sized woodpecker with jet-black plumage, relieved by a scarlet crown and mane in the male and a scarlet nape-patch in the female, inhabits coniferous forests and beechwoods over much of Europe. It can be located by its whistling calls and by its prolonged drumming on dry branches. Large (46cm).

GREEN WOODPECKER
Picus viridis

One hears the ringing, laughing *tew-tew-tewk* of this woodpecker more often than one sees the bird flying in heavy, undulating bounds from tree to tree. It can sometimes be seen stabbing its strong beak vigorously into an anthill and lapping up the occupants with its long, snake-like tongue; or climbing a tree trunk with a series of jerky hops; or 'frozen' motionless when one can admire its olive-green plumage, blood-red crown and canary-yellow rump. Medium (32cm).

LESSER SPOTTED (Barred) WOODPECKER   *Dendrocopus minor*

A sparrow-sized woodpecker found in parks and woods mainly in the southern half of England. It can be identified by its black-and-white barred back, a crimson crown in juveniles and adult males, a whinnying *pee-pee-pee* cry and, during the mating season, by rapid hammering with its beak on a hollow branch or trunk. Small (15cm).

GREATER SPOTTED (Pied) WOODPECKER   *Dendrocopus major*

A resident of both deciduous and conifer woods in England and Wales and found locally to north Scotland. It can be told from the Lesser form by its plain black back, the scarlet under its tail, a scarlet spot on the nape of the male (juveniles have scarlet crowns), prominent white wing-patches, more powerful 'drumming' in shorter bursts and a loud and frequent *tchick* call. Medium (23cm).

WRYNECK   *Jynx torquilla*

An inconspicuous bird with mottled grey-brown plumage which is possibly extinct as a breeding species in Britain but is still a scarce passage visitor. Unless nesting, when its clear thrush-like *quee-quee-quee* is heard, it is difficult to detect as it spends much of its time high in trees. Small (17cm).

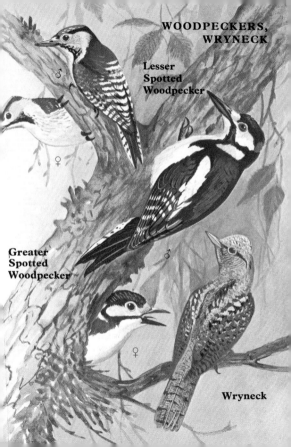

WOODPECKERS, WRYNECK

Lesser Spotted Woodpecker

Greater Spotted Woodpecker

Wryneck

CRESTED LARK *Galerida cristata*

Although this lark breeds throughout central and western Europe right up to the Channel coast very few have been seen in Britain. It inhabits open grassy or arid country from sea level to mountains and is often seen on dusty tracks, sandy fields or urban wasteland. It can be recognised by its very pale sandy-buff plumage, long, narrow, erect crest, rather short tail and the absence of white on its wings and tail. It perches more frequently than the Skylark (p. 144) and sings on the ground and in flight a delicate, high-pitched, often repeated, twittering song of 3 notes – *tzee-zer-wee*. Small (17cm).

SKYLARK *Alauda arvensis*

This bird breeds throughout Britain in open country from sea level to moors and occasionally mountain tops. Few other birds' songs are so widely recognised as the Skylark's trilling notes, which may continue without a break for 2 or 3 or even 5 minutes, as it mounts upwards in tight circles or hangs poised between heaven and earth; it occasionally sings on the ground or a perch. At close quarters its short rounded crest and the conspicuous white on the outer feathers of its longish tail can be seen; it also has a characteristic crouching walk. Small (17cm).

WOOD LARK *Lullula arborea*

Unlike the Skylark, the Wood Lark is found only in the southern half of Britain in thinly wooded country such as commons or heaths where there are some trees on which it can perch; as these habitats disappear it is found in increasingly fewer places. Like the Skylark, Wood Larks also sing on the wing but usually while swinging round in wide circles, and their songs are never continuous but interrupted every few seconds for equally short periods of silence. The song phrases are extremely varied with rich flute-like bubbling trills recalling those of the Song Thrush (p. 168) and especially the Nightingale (p. 160); the Wood Lark sings at any time of day or night. At rest it can be seen to have a much shorter tail than the Skylark, without white on the sides, and is noticeably sandy-coloured with a conspicuous yellow-white eye-stripe. Small (15cm).

Skylark

Wood Lark

SWALLOW   *Hirundo rustica*
After wintering in South Africa, the Swallow returns
early in spring to most cultivated parts of the British
Isles. It is a slender, dark steely-blue bird with a
chestnut-red throat and forehead, and creamy-white
underparts except for a dark-blue breast-band. It
can be identified by its long tail feathers or streamers
(short in juveniles) and forked tail as it sweeps to-
and-fro after insects or skims over a pond to sip
water. Small (19cm).

HOUSE MARTIN   *Delichon urbica*
Like the Swallow the House Martin winters in
southern Africa but returns in spring to all parts of
the British Isles to plaster nests of wet mud pellets
and grass stems under the eaves of houses; some
colonies nest on inland crags and sea cliffs. It can be
distinguished from the Swallow by its white rump
(not always visible in flight), pure white underparts,
white-feathered legs and feet, and its short forked
tail which lacks streamers; juveniles are brownish.
Small (13cm).

SAND MARTIN   *Riparia riparia*
Wintering as far north as East Africa, these martins
return to most parts of the British Isles usually by
late March. It can be distinguished from the House
Martin by its fawnish-brown upperparts and breast-
band, only slightly forked tail, more butterfly-like
flight and its habit of nesting colonially in sand and
gravel pits, banks and even sea cliffs in tunnels up to
1m long. Small (12cm).

SWALLOWS

Swallow

House
Martin

House
Martin

Sand Martin

MEADOW PIPIT *Anthus pratensis*

This insignificantly plumaged, streaked and spotted olive-brown pipit is perhaps the most numerous and widely distributed of all small British birds and is found everywhere from urban wasteland to mountain pastures and remote islands. As with the larks, the safest way to distinguish between the various pipits is by their songs, as many of them share similar plumage and habitats. The Meadow Pipit is characterised by a thin *seep*ing call as it mounts up a metre or so from one's feet to parachute slowly down again with a diminishing and accelerating sequence of tinkling notes to its nest of grasses in a tussock or among the long heather edging a moorland road. If it is not in song, it may be recognised by its call-note and long hind claws. Small (14cm).

TREE PIPIT *Anthus trivialis*

This bird is a summer resident in woods or scattered trees on the edges of commons or moors in many parts of Britain but not in Ireland. It may often be found in similar haunts to those of the Meadow Pipit but it can be identified by its different song flight which usually takes place while flying from and to a high perch in a tree, though it may also sing when it is perching; in addition its song is much more powerful and musical and usually ends in a high-pitched far-carrying *pee-pee-pee*. Outside the breeding season, its harsh call-note distinguishes it from the similarly plumaged Meadow Pipit; at close range it is possible to see its short hind claws and its pink instead of brown legs, though the latter is not a reliable distinction. Small (15cm).

149

TAWNY PIPIT *Anthus campestris*

Although the Tawny Pipit breeds in northern France and Holland and has been known to nest in southern England, it is mainly a very sporadic autumn visitor to Kent and Sussex. It is a slim, pale, sandy-brown bird with long, yellowish legs and a rather conspicuous cream-coloured eye-stripe, and both in its appearance and in its call-note, which is loud and harsh, it resembles a wagtail more than a pipit. It walks and runs very swiftly, moving its tail up and down, and has an undulating flight. In its breeding haunts it is essentially a bird of sandy heaths and dunes, arid pastures and barren, rocky ground sparsely covered with scrub, and nests in depressions in the ground, in large tussocks or clods of earth. Small (16cm).

ROCK PIPIT *Anthus spinoletta*

This bird is exclusively a coastal species though it often nests some distance inland on island moors. In some areas, especially on islands, its habitat may overlap with the Meadow Pipit's (p. 148); however the Rock Pipit can be distinguished in theory (though in the field it is often difficult) by its stronger, more musical song, as it mounts a metre or so in the air before parachuting downwards, and its darker legs and grey instead of white tail feathers. Except during the migratory seasons, a pipit seen on cliffs, rocky seashores, sands or mudflats may normally be safely identified as a Rock Pipit, and no other pipits are likely to be found searching for insects on reefs or in beds of seaweed. Small (16cm).

WAGTAILS

♀

♂
summer

YELLOW WAGTAIL
Motacilla flava

Two forms of this wagtail breed in Britain, though the blue-headed form only nests sporadically in south-east and east England. The more widespread form is a glowing saffron colour with greenish-brown back, the female is paler and browner; it nests in pastures and watermeadows, though also on heaths and commons, locally in England and Wales but it is scarce in Scotland. Dancing up and down after insects disturbed by grazing cattle, the long-legged, long-tailed Yellow Wagtail cannot be mistaken for any other bird; its shrill bell-like call and brief warbling song are also quite distinctive. Small (17cm).

winter

♂

summer

♂

GREY WAGTAIL *Motacilla cinerea*

During the breeding season the Grey Wagtail nests on fast-flowing streams in hilly districts of west and north Britain; it moves south after nesting and visits lowland ponds and streams. It is the most beautiful of the wagtails with its blue-grey head and back, vivid sulphur-yellow underparts and, in the male, a contrasting black gorget (white in winter). It attracts attention by the constant dipping of its very long tail as it trips over boulders in midstream or dances up in shuttle-cock flights after insects, before flying off with long, looping bounds to its mossy nest in a crevice in an old stone bridge or rocky outcrop. Small (18cm).

WAGTAILS

winter

summer

WHITE WAGTAIL
Motacilla alba alba

This is the Continental form of the British Pied Wagtail and although it has occasionally nested in Britain it is predominantly a coastal passage bird. It is often difficult to distinguish between the two forms especially in autumn when many are in immature plumage. In summer, however, the male White Wagtail with black cap and breast and pale grey back contrasts with the sooty-backed male Pied Wagtail; the female Pied Wagtail is greyer on the back and has less black on the head and breast. Small (18cm).

imm.

summer

♂

PIED WAGTAIL
Motacilla alba yarrelli

This bird breeds throughout the British Isles from city centre to the remotest Scottish glen, almost invariably near human habitation and often near water, nesting in such varied sites as farm buildings, pollarded trees, sea cliffs and stone dykes. It can be recognised by its constant unmistakable *tzissick* call and by its lively warbling song when excited. Some Pied Wagtails emigrate to south-west Europe in the winter, others roost in hundreds in plantations, reedbeds or buildings. Small (18cm).

WREN

WREN *Troglodytes troglodytes*
This tiny brown-barred bird with a short up-cocked tail is found in all parts of the British Isles including the oceanic islands of St Kilda in the Hebrides and up to a height of 600m in Highland glens; in the remoter parts of its range, it can be found nesting in cliffs and woods many miles from the nearest habitation which, unlike Robins (p. 160) and Dunnocks (p. 158), it tends to shun. The Wren is more often heard than seen, for, despite its minute size, it has a prolonged stuttering scold and a still more prolonged rattling warbling song of astounding power and vehemence that terminates in an especially emphatic and explosive trill. In flight it whirrs on rapidly vibrating wings for short distances. Very small (9cm).

DIPPER *Cinclus cinclus*

This species is associated with swift hill-streams in the west and north of Britain and builds its large domed nest of moss in a rocky bank or behind a waterfall. Though very like a Wren in form, the Dipper is twice as big and has dark brown, almost black, plumage and a snowy breast with brown bellyband. It may be seen in swift arrow-like flight low over a stream, making a sharp *zit-zit* call, or actually walking under water on the bed of the stream. In quiet reaches its unexpectedly musical warbling song may be heard as it bobs on a boulder or perches on a branch just above the water. Medium small (17cm).

DUNNOCK (Hedge Sparrow)
Prunella modularis

Though almost as common an inhabitant of gardens as the Robin, and frequenting many different habitats from Highland glen to sea cliff, the Dunnock tends to be overlooked. Its plumage is an inconspicuous streaky brown colour with grey head and breast, and it has equally inconspicuous habits, as it threads its way through shrubbery or hedge, hunting for insects, worms and seeds, or creeps about the ground beneath the bird-table, seldom venturing to alight actually on the table. Nor is its warbling ditty of a song, repeated several times a minute, any more noticeable, except when sung unexpectedly in the middle of the night. Only its loud single piping note draws attention to it and its habit of continually shuffling its wings. Small (15cm).

ALPINE ACCENTOR
Prunella collaris

A rare vagrant to the British Isles from the mountains of southern and central Europe where it nests in crevices among the rocks from 1,200m up to the permanent snow level. It is much larger and more brightly coloured than the Dunnock, with a whitish chin and throat spotted with black, chestnut-streaked flanks and a broken double white wing-bar. Its rippling call and lark-like song are also more conspicuous, though in general, apart from its short song-flight, its habits are as unobtrusive as those of the Dunnock. Small (18cm).

NIGHTINGALE *Luscinia megarhynchos*

This small brown bird with a coppery tail is a summer resident mainly in the east and south of England. With its habit of skulking in dense cover, this inconspicuous bird would be rarely noticed were it not for its liquid, bubbling, superbly warbled song and contrasting croaking alarm-call. Although the quality of the song varies greatly from bird to bird, at its best the fluting crescendo throbs until one's pulsing eardrums seem likely to burst with the vibrant waves of song. Medium small (16cm).

BLUETHROAT *Luscinia svecica*

The superb song of the Bluethroat can be heard exceptionally in the Scottish Highlands, but it is normally a regular passage migrant in small numbers along the east coast. Most British visitors are immature birds somewhat resembling young Robins or Nightingales; breeding males from Scandinavia and eastern Europe have a red spot on their bright blue gorgets; in those from central and southern Europe the spot is white. Small (14cm).

ROBIN *Erithacus rubecula*

One may think of the Robin as an exclusively English bird but it is found in almost every part of Britain; moreover, many British-nesting Robins emigrate to Europe in autumn and Scandinavian Robins winter in Britain. No description of the adult Robin is needed; however, the young are spotted and do not acquire the orange-russet breast until the late summer or autumn. Small (14cm).

Night-ingale

NIGHT-INGALE, BLUETHROAT, ROBIN

Red-spotted Bluethroat
autumn

White-spotted Bluethroat
summer

imm.

Robin   adult

STONECHAT *Saxicola torquata*

Although this species is resident throughout the British Isles, especially in coastal areas, it is very local and decreasing in numbers, possibly because many birds die whenever there is a hard winter. The male, 'chatting' and 'wheeting' from the topmost spray of gorse or bramble, is distinguished by a velvety coal-black head, white neck and wing-patches, and terracotta underparts; the female lacks the black-and-white colouring and could be mistaken for a Whinchat. Small (12cm).

WHINCHAT *Saxicola rubetra*

This is a local summer resident on commons, railway embankments, moors and partly wooded valleys in most parts of Britain. It can be distinguished from the female Stonechat by a broad white eye-stripe, black cheeks and white patches near the base of the tail; in addition, its song is a sweet mellow warble in contrast to the Stonechat's simple trill. Small (14cm).

WHEATEAR *Oenanthe oenanthe*

This common summer resident nests all over the British Isles from coastal links to mountain top. It is an unmistakable sandy-coloured bird with a pale grey mantle (brown in the female) and a conspicuous white rump. It characteristically makes short low flights, darts in and out of holes, bobs restlessly about, flirting its black-and-white tail, and hovers a metre or so above the ground while uttering brief snatches of its squeaky song. Small (14cm).

CHATS

Stonechat

♀

♂

Whinchat

♂

♀

Wheatear

♀

♂

BLACK REDSTART
Phoenicurus ochruros

These birds have always been regular passage
visitors but in the last 50 years they have also
started to nest in urban areas in south and east
Britain. Black Redstarts can be recognised by
their brief warbling song ending in a distinctive metallic jingling; male birds have unmistakable inky-black plumage, white wing-
patches and flame-coloured tails, while the
greyer females and immature males can be
distinguished from common Redstarts by the
absence of orange on their underparts. Small
(13cm).

REDSTART *Phoenicurus phoenicurus*
This redstart is mainly a summer resident in woodland in most parts of Britain, though like the Black Redstart it is also a passage visitor. Despite its tropically bright plumage, it is not a conspicuous bird, being always on the move among the leaves, only darting out now and again after a passing insect to display its flame-coloured breast and tail. However, it attracts attention by its loud *phuee* call, its 'ticking' scold and sprightly but disjointed warbling which includes fine notes of Nightingale (p. 160) and Chaffinch (p. 216) quality. Small (14cm).

THRUSHES

BLACKBIRD *Turdus merula*

One of the commonest British birds, found almost anywhere in Britain where there are trees or bushes; in winter, large numbers of immigrants gather on the east coast. Blackbirds are the noisiest of the thrushes especially towards roosting time in winter when their staccato *dik-dik-dik* rivals in persistence pheasants crowing from coverts; however, no bird's song is more musical, mellow or flute-like – though even this superb melody may end in a jarring screech. Both sexes distinctively lift their tails over their backs on alighting. Medium small (25cm).

TLE THRUSH *Turdus viscivorus*

species is found in cultivated country and
s throughout Britain in the breeding season; at
times of the year it wanders in family flocks
owns and moors. It can be distinguished from
ong Thrush (p. 168) by its greyer plumage,
heavily spotted underparts, its white under-
nd white-tipped tail. It is notable for its habit
ging its clear whistling song from the top of a
ee on stormy days; it also attracts attention by
hissing alarm call. Medium (26cm).

RING OUZEL *Turdus torquatus*

This mountain blackbird is a summer resident in
hilly districts in Britain and builds its nest in heather
and under juniper bushes. In some areas, where its
haunts overlap with that of the Blackbird's, it is
possible to confuse the two as the female Ring
Ouzel's gorget is very dull, although it usually has a
greyish tint to its wings. However, the Ring Ouzel's
dashing flight, its harsh stony *chack* call and clear
piping *phwee-phwee-phwee* song, often delivered
from a boulder on the hillside, are all distinctive and
unmistakable. Medium small (23cm).

THRUSHES

SONG THRUSH *Turdus philomelos*
This species is found almost anywhere near habitation in Britain where there are bushes or hedgerows, in which it can nest, and stones, on which to hammer open the shells of snails. It also stands, with its head on one side, looking for worms. After nesting, those birds in hill country, particularly in northern Britain, migrate south. The Song Thrush is olive-brown with a cream-coloured breast flecked with dark-brown spots and streaks; it could not be mistaken during the breeding season for any other bird except the bigger and greyer Mistle Thrush (p. 170). Its varied, powerful song of clear whistles is heard for much of the year. Medium small (22cm).

REDWING *Turdus iliacus*
Although a number of these [ ] nesting in the Scottish Highla[ ] dominantly winter visitors to B[ ] immense numbers from Scandin[ ] the winter ranging in flocks, o[ ] (p. 171), over fields and open w[ ] on worms and berries. They [ ] from Song Thrushes by their pr[ ] stripes, bright russet flanks a[ ] russet under the wings. On a l[ ] flock may be heard warblin[ ] Linnet-like notes (p. 220) and[ ] trills. Medium small (21cm).

FIELDFARE
Turdus pilaris

A few pairs of this thrush are now nesting in the Scottish Highlands and have also been known to nest in the Pennines; but, like the Redwing (p. 169), this species is mainly a winter visitor to Britain's arable lands, fields and thorn hedges. The Fieldfare has a distinctive plumage of greyish-blue head and rump, chestnut mantle, chocolate-brown tail and streaked golden-brown breast; in flight (which is less undulating than the Mistle Thrush's) its underparts have a silvery gleam. Its call is a harsh chuckling *chack*, though migrating birds can make an extraordinary falsetto squeaky *chisseek*. Medium (25cm).

SEDGE WARBLER

Acrocephalus schoenobaenus

This is the most widely distributed of the various
marsh warblers and is found nesting in reedbeds,
hedges and bushes, usually near water, thoughout
Britain. Like all the marsh warblers it is a small
brown skulking bird which seldom leaves shelter and
must be identified by its loud churring call and its
song of harsh, musical and mimicking notes whenever it is disturbed, by day or night. At close range it
can be identified by its whitish eye-stripe and the
dark streaks on its back. Small (12cm).

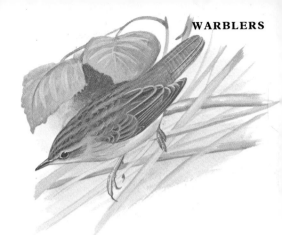

GRASSHOPPER WARBLER

Locustella naevia

This warbler is found breeding in most parts of Britain in marshy land, on commons and on brackeny sites in felled woods. It is so secretive and its plumage so undistinguished that it must be identified by its unique song – an interminable high-pitched reeling trill which rises and falls as the bird turns its head from side to side. Sometimes the song is almost inaudible, sometimes it carries 500m; it cannot be mistaken for any other common British bird's song, except possibly a Nightjar's (p. 127), though it might be confused with an insect's. Small (12cm).

WARBLERS

CETTI'S WARBLER *Cettia cettia*

A series of mild winters in the 1940s and 1950s encouraged this warbler to extend its breeding range to reedbeds and thickets in northern France, the Channel Islands and Kent. It is another skulking warbler and is rarely in the open for more than a few seconds, although if it has eggs or nestlings, it may uncharacteristically approach to within a metre or so of an intruder. With its unremarkable dark rufous colour, dull whitish eye-stripe and greyish underparts, it is normally only detected by its sudden forceful *prrree* call or very loud explosive 4-note song of Blackcap (p. 180) quality. Small (14cm).

SAVI'S WARBLER

Locustella luscinioides

After becoming extinct in Britain in the last century when the Fens were drained, this warbler has started to nest again in small numbers in several places in southern England where there are swamps and reedbeds with scattered bushes. Though not so secretive as some other marsh warblers, it too is located by its song. This resembles the Grasshopper Warbler's (p. 173) but is lower-pitched and does not reel on and on and may be preceded by low ticking notes that accelerate into the reeling; its plumage is uniformly rufous, not streaked like the Grasshopper Warbler's. Small (14cm).

REED WARBLER   *Acrocephalus scirpaceus*
This marshland warbler nests mainly in the southern half of England. Like the Sedge Warbler (p. 172), its frequent neighbour, its plumage is not streaked but it can be immediately distinguished by the absence of the prominent eye-stripe. The 2 warblers' songs are similar and both are sustained for several seconds or even minutes at a time; however, the Reed Warbler's more even and musical warbling lacks the Sedge Warbler's extraordinary variety. Small (12cm).

GREAT REED WARBLER
A. arundinaceus
This giant reed warbler, not much smaller than a Starling, rarely wanders to Britain as there are no extensive reedbeds in which it can nest. Its size is usually sufficient to identify it from the small Reed Warbler but it also has a markedly long straight beak and in most cases an eye-stripe. In addition, it has a distinctive strident *chack-chack* call and a powerful gutteral croaking song which can be heard at a considerable distance. Small (19cm).

MARSH WARBLER   *A. palustris*
This bird is a scarce summer resident in some parts of the southern Midlands and the south-west where it usually nests in ditches and osier beds with trees. Its plumage is hardly distinguishable from the Reed Warbler's but its more vivacious and musical song leaves little doubt as to its identity; it is an even more prolific mimic than the Sedge Warbler (p. 172) but it usually omits the latter's harsh notes. Small (12cm).

WARBLERS

Reed Warbler

Great Reed Warbler

Marsh Warbler

WARBLERS

WHITETHROAT *Sylvia communis*

This summer resident has recently become scarce in
parts of England; however, in normal summers, this
warbler's harsh 'pebbly' scolding *churr* from the
depths of the hedge or nettlebed in which it is skulking, and its excitable chattering warble as it tosses
itself up into the air, are familiar features of summer
in most parts of Britain where there is a 'jungly' growth
of brambles, briars, bushes and hedges, or clearings
at the edge of woods. Both male and female Whitethroat are rusty brown with more rufous wings but
the male has a pure white throat, bushy grey cap and
white outer tail-feathers. The female nests in thick
cover such as overgrown hedgerows and rough wasteland a metre or so above the ground. Small (13cm).

LESSER WHITETHROAT *Sylvia curruca*

This species is a much more local summer resident than the Whitethroat and becomes increasingly scarcer towards Scotland; however, since it seldom leaves cover it must often be overlooked. The Lesser Whitethroat frequents similar but taller hedges than the Whitethroat, preferably with trees, and also large gardens, and nests in similar situations. However, the Lesser Whitethroat can be distinguished by its blackish-grey ear-coverts, greyer upperparts and by the lack of rufous markings on the wings. Its song, delivered mainly from cover and not in flight, is quite different – a loud 4- or 5-note Cirl Bunting-like rattle (p. 229) standing out from an often inaudible warbling. Small (13cm).

WARBLERS

♀

♂

BLACKCAP *Sylvia atricapilla*
This is a summer resident mainly in English woods
and shrubberies but it is known to breed as far north
as the Scottish Highlands; individuals occasionally
winter in southern Britain. The Blackcap is one of
the classic songsters, pouring out a wild piping of
wonderfully loud and sustained flute-like notes
(similar in tone to the Blackbird's, p. 166) which
terminate abruptly when the melody is at its most
exuberant. Its song is unsurpassed in richness and
vivacity, though it usually sings from dense cover
and seldom perches with deliberate intent to sing.
It can be recognised by its ash-grey and brown plumage with a glossy coal-black crown; the female
has a copper-brown cap. Small (14cm).

GARDEN WARBLER *Sylvia borin*
Like the Blackcap, this species is another summer visitor to English woodlands with thick undergrowth. Although its song is similar to the Blackcap's it is more sustained and a Garden Warbler may sing almost without a break for as long as 5 minutes. It has notably black eyes. Small (14cm).

BARRED WARBLER *Sylvia nisoria*
This is an autumn passage migrant to the east coast, at which season it lacks the distinctive yellow eye and barred underparts of summer. Small (15cm).

Garden Warbler

Barred Warbler
autumn

WARBLERS

WOOD WARBLER
Phylloscopus sibilatrix

This warbler is found in beech, oak and birchwoods in many parts of Britain but is never very numerous. Although it builds its domed nest of bracken, leaves and grasses in a hollow in the ground, it is not often seen as it spends most of its time in the upper part of trees and is often difficult to locate as it does not sing as frequently as most 'leaf' warblers. Its song however is unmistakable, being a stuttering ticking note that accelerates into a single plaintive *tewee*. Its yellow-green upperparts, sulphurous throat and breast and pure white underparts are also distinctive. Small (12cm).

ICTERINE WARBLER *Hippolais icterina*

This warbler is increasingly often reported from coastal migration stations and is known to have nested in Britain; indeed, there is no reason why it should not nest here more often as it is found in parks and gardens as well as woods and hedgerows on the Continent. It resembles a heavily built Wood Warbler but can be identified by its bright lemon-yellow (not white) belly and blue-grey legs and its habit of erecting its crown-feathers when excited which gives its head a steep-browed appearance. Its harsh song recalls both the Nightingale's (p. 160) and the Marsh Warbler's (p. 176) but the jumble of notes, each repeated several times, includes both musical and extraordinarily discordant ones. Small (13cm).

CHIFFCHAFF *Phylloscopus collybita*

This tiny greenish-yellow warbler nests as far north as the Scottish Lowlands. It is often not easy to differentiate Chiffchaffs from Willow Warblers as they flit among the foliage, but at close range the Chiffchaff's legs appear almost black and the Willow Warbler's are usually pale brown. However, Chiffchaffs prefer woods with larger trees as they do not sing from trees less than about 5m high, while their song is unmistakable and, in the nesting season, one has only to wait a few minutes before hearing the monotonous repetitive *chiff-chaff-chaff-chiff-chiff*. Very small (10cm).

WILLOW WARBLER
Phylloscopus trochilus

In contrast to the Chiffchaff, this warbler is found in large numbers all over the British Isles wherever there are thickets or trees. Its lisping call of wistful tinkling notes is the most delicately sweet and most persistently repeated of all the songs of summer, though when displaying to its mate, or anxious at the presence of a Cuckoo (p. 126) near its nest, a Willow Warbler utters an uncharacteristically loud *pee-pee-pee* as it stretches upwards and fans its wings feverishly; its call-note, a soft *hooeet*, is similar to the Chiffchaff's. The Willow Warbler's neat domed nest is more compactly constructed than a Chiffchaff's and is actually built on the ground, whereas Chiffchaffs build their nests a metre or so above the ground on a base of dead leaves in a clump of brambles or thick undergrowth. Very small (10cm).

GOLDCREST

GOLDCREST *Regulus regulus*

Resident in mainly coniferous woods throughout Britain, where it can suspend its hammock nest of mosses woven with spiders' webs from a branch; it is also a numerous autumn immigrant to the east coast. Practice is needed to distinguish its needle-thin bat-like call from a Coal Tit's note, though its equally high-pitched and persistently reiterated reeling song is unmistakable. In dull light it may be impossible to see its greenish plumage, two whitish wing-bars and orange crest (pale yellow in the female), but its size distinguishes it from all other birds except the Firecrest. Very small (9cm).

FIRECREST *Regulus ignicapillus*

Previously only scarce winter visitors, in recent years Firecrests have regularly crossed the Channel to nest in bushes and low trees, rather than conifer woods, in southern England. Although resembling the Goldcrest in form, its olive-green plumage has a distinctly yellowish tinge, heightened by a bronze sheen on the nape and shoulders; but it is most immediately distinguished from the Goldcrest by its broad whitish-fawn stripe above the eye and a black stripe through it. In addition, the crests are different colours – the female's copper-gold, the male's flame-coloured; and the song is louder, lower-pitched, less persistent and hardly more than a repetition of one note. Very small (9cm).

FLYCATCHERS

SPOTTED FLYCATCHER
Muscicapa striata

A summer visitor from Africa which is found in small numbers in all parts of Britain from town park to Highland glen, nesting on a branch or the beam of a building. With its streaky, nondescript plumage, its thin piping call and its infrequent soft twittering song it is an inconspicuous bird except for its habit of perching on a dead branch or tennis net and making constant short fluttering flights after passing insects. Small (14cm).

PIED FLYCATCHER   *Ficedula hypoleuca*

A summer resident which nests in holes in oak, birch and alder trees mainly in wooded valleys in Wales and the Scottish Border counties, where it may be seen darting out from a tree after an insect; also in spring and autumn on the coast when migrating. The male can be distinguished from the Spotted Flycatcher by its conspicuous pied plumage, with black satiny mantle, white forehead, large white wing-patch and snow-white underparts; the female is a drab olive-brown. Its song is of little help in locating it, since phrases of it could be attributed to the Redstart, Robin, Pied Wagtail, Reed Bunting and even the Great Tit. Small (13cm).

BEARDED TIT *Panurus biarmicus*
The number of Bearded Tits in Britain depends on the severity or mildness of the winter and also on the extent of saltwater flooding in the reedbeds it inhabits; mild winters enable it to build up its population in East Anglian fenland but a very severe weather may reduce it to near-extinction. When present it attracts attention by its bell-like *ping-ping* call as it flies over the reeds on short, rounded, rapidly whirring wings with black-and-white bars. Its body and long tail are tawny orange and the male has an ash-grey head and conspicuous black mustachios. Small (16cm).

LONG-TAILED TIT *Aegithalos caudatus*

This tit, found in copses and hedgerows throughout Britain, is able to survive hard winters better than the Bearded Tit even in Highland glens up to 500m. With its tail longer than the remainder of its body and a delicate rosy tint to its black-and-white plumage this is one of the easiest of the woodland tits to recognise; while the stuttering *zip-zip-zip* of a dozen Long-tailed Tits fluttering with undulating flight one after another from tree to tree is one of the most distinctive of tit calls. Its marvellous oval nest made of moss woven together with cobwebs and hair, covered with lichens and lined with as many as 2,000 feathers, is usually built in gorse, thorn or bramble bushes. There is space within this nest for 10 or 20 nestlings. Small (13cm; tail 7cm).

MARSH TIT *Parus palustris*
This species is mainly a local resident in England and Wales. The Marsh and Willow Tits are the 2 most difficult British tits to differentiate as they are both small brown-backed birds with black caps; the Marsh Tit's cap usually has a bluish gloss but this is seldom obvious in the field. Unlike the Willow Tit, it rarely excavates its own nesting hole in a tree; its nest is lined with a foundation of moss and a thick pad of rabbit's fur. Its 2-noted *tzervee* call resembles the Coal Tit's (p. 195) and some musical song notes may occasionally be heard. Very small (11cm).

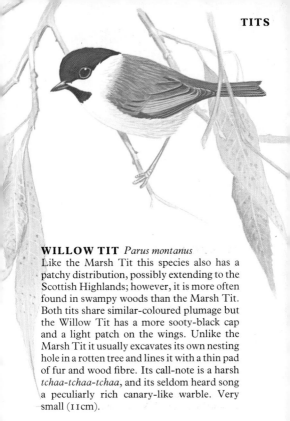

WILLOW TIT *Parus montanus*
Like the Marsh Tit this species also has a
patchy distribution, possibly extending to the
Scottish Highlands; however, it is more often
found in swampy woods than the Marsh Tit.
Both tits share similar-coloured plumage but
the Willow Tit has a more sooty-black cap
and a light patch on the wings. Unlike the
Marsh Tit it usually excavates its own nesting
hole in a rotten tree and lines it with a thin pad
of fur and wood fibre. Its call-note is a harsh
tchaa-tchaa-tchaa, and its seldom heard song
a peculiarly rich canary-like warble. Very
small (11cm).

CRESTED TIT *Parus cristatus*

Though this brown-backed tit's range extends over most of Europe, it is found only extremely locally in Britain in some pine forests of the Scottish Highlands. It nests in holes in decaying trees but is often seen flitting down to pick up a grub or insect from the heather. It can be distinguished from its inseparable companion, the Coal Tit, by its unique shovel-shaped speckled bluish-grey crest and intensely black triangular gorget, and also by its musical purring trill. Its infrequently heard song is as unusual as the Willow Tit's (p. 193), being a sweet and brilliant warble of 7 or 10 notes. Very small (11cm).

COAL TIT *Parus ater*

This olive-grey tit with whitish-buff underparts is the second smallest British breeding bird. It inhabits woods throughout the British Isles, especially coniferous woods where it often accompanies Goldcrests (p. 186), but it is less common at bird-tables in gardens and parks than Blue and Great Tits. It can be distinguished from the Great Tit (p. 196) by its smaller size, its black throatband which does not extend down the belly, and its sweeter, less metallic, more rapid *chuvee, chuvee* from the Great Tit's ringing *ee-hew, ee-hew*. In addition the white spot at the nape of its black neck distinguishes it from the Marsh and Willow Tits (pp. 192–3), as well as the Great Tit; however, in juvenile and Irish Coal Tits the whitish markings are yellowish. Very small (10cm).

BLUE TIT *Parus caeruleus*

Seven species of woodland tits (pp. 191–6) nest in Britain and various combinations of these may be seen in the mixed insect-hunting winter flocks. Blue Tits and Great Tits will be familiar to everyone, as visitors to bird-tables and also to milk bottles with tinfoil tops, in all parts of the British Isles, though they are scarce in north-west Scotland. Only the Blue Tit has a bright cobalt-blue crown, wings and tail, white cheeks and yellow underparts, though young ones have greenish-brown upperparts and yellow cheeks. Nor does any other tit's song resemble the Blue Tit's bell-like trilling, though its harsh scolding *churr-r-r* can be confused with the similar scold of the Great Tit. Very small (11cm).

GREAT TIT *Parus major*

This common visitor to suburban bird-tables has approximately the same range in Britain as the Blue Tit; there is also some immigration of both species from Europe. The Great Tit, with its greenish blue-grey back, cannot be mistaken for any other tit, for, in addition to being the largest, it has a broad black band extending from its glossy blue-black head and throat down the centre of its bright yellow breast and belly; even the browner-black and whiter-yellow juvenile is distinctive. Its various call-notes may be confused with those of other tits but the silvery axe-blows of its song are usually much louder than those of the Coal Tit (p. 195). Small (14cm).

TITS

Blue Tit

Great Tit

TREE CREEPER *Certhia familiaris*

Tree Creepers are well distributed in coniferous and deciduous woods from English parks to remotest Highland glens, but though they often accompany roving bands of tits, one rarely sees more than 3 or 4 together. It is characteristically seen creeping rapidly up and round the bole of a tree, supported by its stiff tail, while probing with its long curved beak into every crevice for insects, spiders or woodlice; then, with a gleam of silvery undersides, it flits down to the base of another tree and swarms up it. The Tree Creeper's song is a rather louder variant of the Goldcrest's (p. 186), repeated at intervals, and its shrill drawn-out *tsee-ee* call-note is a familiar sound in woods. Small (12cm).

NUTHATCH *Sitta europaea*

This species is found in woods and gardens mainly in the southern half of Britain. The Nuthatch's clear thrush-like whistles and merry bubbling calls are unmistakable; and its blue-grey back, the black stripe through its eye and pinkish underparts are usually fairly conspicuous as it leaps jerkily up the trunk of a tree, or with equal facility, head-first down it. It is mainly a nut-eater, particularly hazel nuts which it wedges in crevices and pickaxes open with blows of its strong sharp beak. With this tool it also plasters up its nest-hole with mud until the entrance is too small for larger birds, such as Starlings (p. 213), that might appropriate it. Small (14cm).

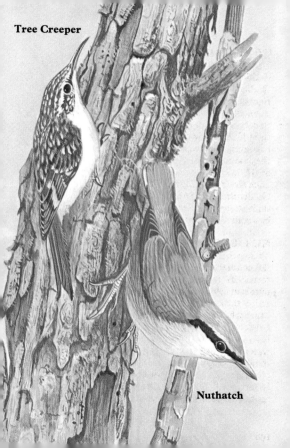

Tree Creeper

Nuthatch

RED-BACKED SHRIKE
Lanius collurio

Now a scarce summer resident in southern England. The chestnut-backed male with its black-and-white tail and black eye-stripe through its blue-grey head, swoops down from telegraph wires in pursuit of insects or a small bird. The brown female makes a harsh croaking. Medium small (17cm).

GREAT GREY SHRIKE
L. excubitor

An uncommon, usually solitary winter visitor. With its pale grey plumage, black-and-white wings and long white-tipped tail it resembles a small Cuckoo (p. 126) or Magpie (p. 204) in flight. It has a hooked beak, a bold black eye-stripe, and a huge head which appears too heavy for its slender body. Medium (23cm).

WOODCHAT SHRIKE *L. senator*

This is a very irregular spring visitor mainly to southern England. It is an unmistakable bird with a chestnut head and a white breast; in flight its white rump and shoulder-patches contrast with its black back. Like the Red-backed Shrike, it spikes the small birds and insects it captures on thorns. Medium small (17cm).

SHRIKES

Red-backed Shrike

♂

♀

Great Grey Shrike

Woodchat Shrike

WAXWING

Bombycilla garrulus

This is an uncommon but regular winter visitor to Britain from the forests of northern Europe, and often arrives in large numbers on the east coast in severe weather, spreading extensively inland. A small flock may be found feeding on a bush of scarlet hips or haws. The birds are fearless, and have lavender-brown plumage with long, gauzy, pinkish-chestnut crests blown up over their heads, and brilliant yellow tips to their short, squarish tails. The curious scarlet 'wax' tips on the wings are not always conspicuous – Waxwings fly high, and the only view may be of a starling-like bird flying from the top of a tall tree, with intermittent wing-beats. But it can still be identified by its sibilant trilling call or musical buzzing, which, if the bird is alarmed, changes to a prolonged, shrill, bell-like note. Medium small (17cm).

NUTCRACKER

Nucifraga caryocatactes

This is a very rare autumn vagrant mainly to south and east England from European coniferous forests. Its dark brown, white-speckled plumage distinguishes it from the rest of the crow family, though its dipping flight on very broad blackish wings resembles that of the Jay, and the broad white border to the tail and white under-coverts are then conspicuous. Medium large (31cm).

Waxwing

Nutcracker

MAGPIE *Pica pica*

Magpies are found throughout the British Isles, except in the far north, in such widely different habitats as the fox-covert and field country of the shires, the combes and downs of the south-west and the northern dales. It is a conspicuous black-and-white bird – the black parts glossed with greens, blues and purples – with a very long tail which renders it unmistakable when it takes wing; it has a harsh chattering call. Magpies are usually seen in twos or threes but may collect in larger numbers to roost or display. Medium large (45cm).

JAY *Garrulus glandarius*

This exotically coloured crow is exclusively found in woodland and timbered parkland, mainly in England and Wales. However, its claret colouring, pale blue eyes, blue-and-white wings, white rump and black tail are not often seen as the Jay habitually skulks in the heart of woods and seldom ventures out. It usually betrays its presence by raucous squawks, though in spring assemblies of Jays also utter extraordinary medleys of mewings, croonings and gurglings, interspersed with falsetto mimicries of other birds' calls. Medium large (33cm).

CROWS

Chough

Alpine Chough

CHOUGH *Pyrrhocorax pyrrhocorax*

Here and there on west coast cliffs, quarries and hills in Wales, the Isle of Man, the Inner Hebrides and especially in Ireland, one can still watch small colonies of these now rare birds performing aerobatics or soaring buoyantly on upcurved finger-spaced primaries. Choughs can be recognised by their purple-black plumage, red legs and dark red sharply-curved beaks with which they turn over dung-pats and stones in search of insects, worms or beetles or dig for ants in short coastal turf. Their clear musical cries are higher-pitched than the familiar *tchacks* of Jackdaws (p. 208) which may be nesting in the same locality. Medium large (39cm).

ALPINE CHOUGH *Pyrrhocorax graculus*

There is no accepted record of this mountain bird visiting Britain from its haunts in the Spanish sierras, the Alps and the Balkans; however, it is distinguished from the resident British Chough by its much shorter, only slightly curved, yellow beak. orange or coral-red legs and by its penetrating trilling whistle. In the Alps these Choughs assemble in flocks of up to 1,000 at winter ski-resorts where they may be seen performing fantastic aerobatics or scavenging around hotels and restaurant picnic tables for scraps; they also visit car parks on mountain passes and characteristically follow climbers to the summits. They sometimes nest in chalets and cable-railway huts, though normally in caves and holes in crags. Medium large (37cm).

CROWS

JACKDAW *Corvus monedula*

Jackdaws are found throughout the British Isles in towns, countryside and by the sea; they invariably associate with Rooks in fields and may nest in trees, occasionally in old Rooks' nests, with colonies of Rooks. However, the majority of Jackdaws build their own nests in ruined castles and abbeys, in woods with old timber, or in cliffs or crags. They are easily recognised by their small size, the dark grey to off-white hood, pale grey glassy eye and high-pitched *tchack* call. Flight and gait movements are much quicker than Rooks'. Medium large (29cm).

ROOK *Corvus frugilegus*
The Rook is found throughout the British Isles, typi-cally in flocks of hundreds or thousands feeding on fields and ploughed land or cawing in tree rookeries which in eastern Scotland may include more than 1,000 nests. It can be distinguished from the Carrion Crow (p. 210) by its grey-black beak, the bare patch round the base of the beak and throat, its baggy 'trousers' and rolling gait; juveniles lack the bare whitish face and are best distinguished by more pointed beaks, and the purple sheen on their black plumage. Medium large (45cm).

RAVEN *Corvus corax*

This enormous crow with a heavy shaggy head and massive beak is now restricted to western coastal areas of Britain and the Scottish Highlands. Although it is very much larger than the Rook (p. 209) or crows below, it could be mistaken for one at a distance; on the wing it can be identified by its direct, fast, often soaring flight, usually at a considerable height, and by its trick of intermittently rolling over onto its back with its wings half closed. It is usually seen in family parties and is a noisy bird constantly uttering its deep croaking *prook-prook*. Large (62cm).

CARRION CROW *Corvus corone corone*

This crow is found throughout England, Wales and lowland Scotland usually in pairs or family parties; it is a solitary and secretive nester in the forks of trees and on cliff ledges. It can be distinguished from the Rook (p. 209) by its unfeathered legs, heavier black beak, and the green gloss to its black plumage; it hops rather than walks and its call is a harsh *kraa-kraa*. Medium large (46cm).

HOODED CROW *Corvus corone cornix*

This species replaces the Carrion Crow in Ireland, the Isle of Man and the Scottish Highlands though it interbreeds where their habitats overlap; it is a winter visitor to eastern counties. Medium large (46cm).

CROWS

Raven

Carrion Crow

Hooded Crow

ORIOLE

GOLDEN ORIOLE *Oriolus oriolus*

Most Golden Orioles recorded in Britain are rare spring migrants on east and south coasts and are in immature plumage – yellowish-green with lightly streaked greyish underparts – resembling the female. Adult male Orioles are sulphur yellow with black wings and tail but, even when they breed occasionally in old orchards or well-timbered parks with groves of holm oaks in southern England, they usually remain hidden in the tree-tops and are rarely seen. Their loud fluty mellow whistling song and harsh Jay-like (p. 205) alarm-notes are however unmistakable. Medium (23cm).

STARLING *Sturnus vulgaris*

Although this small bird with its spangled iridescent plumage (young birds are plain brown with whitish throats) has colonised the remotest islands around Britain, it is most familiar in towns and villages. It is characteristically seen uttering its piercing catcalls and musical mimicries of other birds' songs while shivering its wings and ruffling its shaggy throat-feathers; or swarming in tens of thousands above the vast roosts on buildings, plantations, and reedbeds. Medium small (21cm).

summer

winter

SPARROWS

TREE SPARROW *Passer montanus*

In some years substantial numbers of Tree Sparrows from the Continent winter in Britain, but this sparrow is best known as a widely distributed rural breeding bird mainly in east Britain and the Midlands. Hollow trees, especially pollard willows, in the wooded fringes of marshes or sewage farms are favourite sites for nesting holes although nesting colonies are extremely localised. It can be recognised by its round copper-coloured crown, small black bib and white collar, and also by its whistling call which is higher-pitched and less metallic than the House Sparrow's chirrups. Like the House Sparrow it feeds on grain and insects but never raids cornfields in enormous flocks. Small (14cm).

HOUSE SPARROW *Passer domesticus*

Although their garrulous twittering and chirping is
very familiar in towns, House Sparrows have, like
Starlings (p. 213), colonised the remotest parts of
Britain, including islands in the Hebrides and even
in Shetland. However, whether they are on islands or
300m up in the hills, these sparrows rarely nest more
than a kilometre or so away from human habitation,
stuffing their untidy nests of straw into convenient
holes under the eaves of houses, in ivy creeper or
stackyards, or even sometimes in the sides of Rooks'
(p. 209) or Magpies' (p. 204) nests. The male House
Sparrow has a dark grey crown and a ragged black
throat; the female and juvenile are a dingy brown.
Small (14cm).

CHAFFINCH *Fringilla coelebs*

This, the commonest British land bird, is found in villages and farmsteads throughout Britain. With its slate-blue head, pink breast and snowy-white shoulder and wing-patches, the male Chaffinch cannot be mistaken for any other British bird; the female is mainly greenish in colour but is also distinguished by white shoulder 'flashes'. In spring, the Chaffinch's metallic *pink* call and short bursts of rollicking song can be heard the day long from gardens, hedges and woodland copses. Small (15cm).

♀

♂

winter

BRAMBLING *Fringilla montifringilla*

This species often flies over with enormous flocks of
hundreds or thousands of Chaffinches from Scandinavian forests to winter in Britain; it may also be seen
feeding in self-contained flocks in stackyards and
beechwoods. In general appearance Bramblings resemble Chaffinches but can be distinguished in flight
by a narrow white rump slit. The male can also be
recognised by its blackish-brown head and unusual
orange-buff shoulder patches and breast; the female
by its buffish breast. Small (14cm).

SISKIN *Carduelis spinus*

The yellow-grey Siskin nests predominantly in conifers in the Scottish Highlands and in Ireland; it is rather a local winter visitor in small mixed flocks with Redpolls (p. 220) to riverside alder and birch trees in other parts of Britain. With its vivid gold wing-bars and tail edges, it could be described as a tiny Greenfinch (p. 222), though the male Siskin has a black crown and chin. Very small (12cm).

SERIN *Serinus serinus*

After a slow spread north-westwards over Europe, the tiny yellowish Serin has at last begun to nest in southern England. It differs from the male Siskin by its canary-like song and the absence of black markings, from the female Siskin by its stubby beak; and Siskins are not found in the Serin's urban habitat of parks and gardens. Very small (11cm).

CROSSBILL *Loxia curvirostra*

Two races breed in Britain: one locally in East Anglia and Ireland, the other more numerously in pine forests and larch groves in the Highlands. Large numbers of Continental Crossbills may also invade all parts of Britain in summer. The rosy-red males, orange-brown immature males, yellowish-green females and streaked grey-green juveniles are unmistakable; however, the twisted mandibles, with which they wrench out the seeds from larch, spruce and pine cones, are not always obvious as they usually feed at a considerable height, swinging upside down like little parrots. Medium small (16cm).

FINCHES

Serin ♂

Siskin ♂

Crossbill ♂

♀

REDPOLL *Carduelis flammea*

This small finch nests locally in colonies in most parts of Britain, particularly in Scotland and Ireland. Although it has a crimson forehead and breast, black chin and pink rump to set off its streaky brown back and silvery undersides, it is not always easy to separate it from accompanying Siskins (p. 218) in the dim light of woods; however, its tail is noticeably longer and more forked and a flock's sibilant twittering is distinctive. Very small (12cm).

TWITE *Carduelis flavirostris*

This is a moorland and coastal finch which nests in stone dykes or heather; in the crofting villages of the western Highlands and Ireland it more or less replaces the Linnet. Except for its rose-buff throat and the male's pink rump, it is inconspicuously coloured and the best clue to its identity is the small round head, contrasting with the plump brown body and tawny underparts; in winter the beak is noticeably yellow. Small (13cm).

LINNET *Carduelis cannabina*

In summer this species is found in gorse commons, hedgerows and gardens in the less wild regions of Britain; in autumn and winter flocks frequent all kinds of rough ground, including stubble and saltings. The Linnet is larger than the similarly plumaged Redpoll, with, in the breeding season, a grey head with crimson crown, crimson breast and chestnut-brown mantle. Linnets attract attention by their seasonally late choral singing. Small (13cm).

FINCHES

Redpoll ♀ ♂

Linnet ♀ ♂

Twite

FINCHES

GREENFINCH *Carduelis chloris*

This species is found in most parts of the British Isles throughout the year, and is even more conspicuous than the Chaffinch (p. 216) when a compact band of males whirr up from a mixed flock of finches on stubble. Male Greenfinches are plump olive-green birds, the females slightly duller, with distinctive golden bars on the wings and the outside edges of their short cleft tails; in autumn their stout seed-cracking beaks and heads are stained purple with blackberry juice. Their bell-like chirrupings and lazy sleepy *doowee* and nasal *tswee* notes are noisily distinctive in spring; from time to time the males may also be seen circling in bat-like flight and twittering songs of chirrups and trills. Small (14cm).

BULLFINCH *Pyrrhula pyrrhula*

Although this British resident is unmistakable with
its black cap, blue-grey mantle, hunting-pink underparts (much paler in the female) and black wings and
tail, it is a shy bird and surprisingly seldom seen. It
inhabits orchards, gardens, shrubberies and woodlands and is nearly always in family parties; however,
a whispered high-pitched piping is often the first
indication of its presence before it dives into the
undergrowth with a flash of white rump. Its low
warbling song is rarely heard. Small (14cm).

HAWFINCH *Coccothraustes coccothraustes*
This shy bird is found locally throughout most of
England and southern Scotland. With its plump
body and triangular wings it resembles a Starling
(p. 213) but no other bird has such an enormous
square head and massive pink-white or steel-blue
kernel-crushing beak; its plumage is ruddy-brown
with blue-black wings, white 'shoulders' and a short
square flame-coloured tail with white tips. Hawfinches are silent birds, though the male has a 2-
noted song not unlike the Bullfinch's (p. 223); the
call is a thin *seep*. Medium small (17cm).

GOLDFINCH *Carduelis carduelis*

This species of finch is found on wasteland with thistles – it feeds on the seeds – in the less wild regions of Britain south of the Scottish Highlands; it nests in orchards and large gardens. The Goldfinch is the most exquisitely coloured of small British birds with a strikingly banded black, white and ruby-red head and brilliant gold and black wings. Its song, from high perches in trees, is sprightly, higher-pitched than the Greenfinch's (p. 222) and ends in a canary-like trill. 'Charms' of Goldfinch sometimes mingle with the immense flocks of finches found on stubble. Small (12cm).

winter

LAPLAND BUNTING
Calcarius lapponicus

Although this species is a regular autumn and spring bird of passage to north and east coast observatories in Britain, it is rarely seen elsewhere except sometimes on hills inland. In breeding plumage the male has a black head and breast like a Reed Bunting (p. 230) but it can be distinguished by the whitish stripe curving back from the eye and the bright chestnut nape; these colours are obscured in autumn migrants. The female resembles a female Reed Bunting except for 2 pale stripes on the back. Lapland Buntings have a characteristic habit of running. The call-note is a rattling whistle. Small (15cm).

winter

SNOW BUNTING *Plectrophenax nivalis*
These buntings are regular winter visitors to
coastal beaches and stubble fields, and inland
moors and valleys; a few pairs nest irregularly
on the highest mountains in the Highlands.
The winter flocks of several hundred or
thousand birds can be recognised by their
musical bell-like notes and their habit of flying
persistently round and round with a harsh in-
sect-like twittering, intermittently changing
direction and swooping as one bird down to
ground level. Male Snow Buntings are easy to
recognise as they run swiftly over the sand
because of the large amounts of white on the
wings, tails and underparts; the females are
smaller and browner. Small (16cm).

BUNTINGS

YELLOWHAMMER *Emberiza citrinella*

This brilliantly coloured bunting is still the typical hedgerow, heath, farmland and stackyard bird in many parts of Britain, feeding on the ground and nesting in hedge bottoms or bushes, although it is becoming uncommon in some areas. The cock is unmistakable with its mustard-yellow head and breast gleaming in the sun, while it wheezes out its equally unmistakable 'little-bit-of-bread-and-no-cheese' from hedge top or telegraph wire. The duller-plumaged female is distinguished from the Cirl and Corn Buntings (p. 232) by its slimmer build, yellow underparts, bright chestnut rump and white on the outer feathers of the cleft tail. Small (16cm).

CIRL BUNTING *Emberiza cirlus*

This bunting breeds locally in southern and especially south-west England in hedgerows and hedge trees. Its song, delivered from high up in a tree, differs from other buntings' and includes a rattling trill almost identical to that of a Lesser Whitethroat (p. 179); however, the Cirl Bunting has the characteristic stuttering delivery of buntings and sings with its head thrown back. The male is distinctively plumaged with an olive-green and yellow head and face, black throat and olive-green breast-band; the female could be confused with a female Yellowhammer but has an olive-brown instead of chestnut rump. Small (16cm).

REED BUNTING *Emberiza schoeniclus*

This bunting is usually found near water in all parts of the British Isles as it feeds chiefly on the seeds of marsh plants and nests in marshy places, when it may crawl along the ground feigning injury if disturbed; in winter it also frequents fields of stubble and rootcrops. In its nesting haunts the male may be heard repeating its monotonous staccato apology of a song while it clings to a reed, continually spreading and closing its tail and flicking its wings. It can be recognised by a black head and white collar, the brown female by a buff eye-stripe and dark moustache-like streaks. Small (15cm).

ORTOLAN BUNTING
Emberiza hortulana

Small numbers of these buntings are passage visitors to eastern and southern coasts in spring and autumn *en route* to breed in Europe or to winter in the Mediterranean. Its breeding haunts vary; in some regions it is mainly restricted to hills or mountains, in others to plains. The adult male can be recognised by its greyish olive-green head and breast, pale yellow throat with an olive moustache-like streak and pinkish-buff underparts; the female is much duller. At close range the yellowish-white ring around the eye and the pink beak are distinctive in both sexes. Small (16cm).

BUNTINGS

CORN BUNTING *Emberiza calandra*
This, the largest of the buntings, breeds locally in scattered colonies throughout the British Isles usually in open cornlands. In some locations the male's wheezing song, jingling like a bunch of keys, is reiterated ceaselessly throughout the day in summer, from a telegraph wire, hedge top or clod of earth. Except for its heavy build and low labouring flight with legs hanging down, the Corn Bunting has no features to distinguish it, for its plumage is a nondescript streaky drab brown without white on the wings or tail. Small (17cm).

ROCK BUNTING *Emberiza cia*

This south European bunting has only been seen
half-a-dozen times in Britain, though it must be said
that it is an unobtrusive bird; in southern Europe it
inhabits rocky ground with sparse gorse scrub and
heath and scattered pine trees, or hillside vineyards
with loosely-built stone walls, from sea level to
2,350m. The male's ash-grey breast and head with
thin black stripes distinguishes it from other British
buntings; and its reddish-buff belly, streaked chestnut back and habit of flicking open its tail when
feeding on the ground to reveal its conspicuous white
feathers are also distinctive. The female is duller
with less defined head markings. Small (15cm).

233

Index of English Names

235

Index of Scientific Names

239